# FALLING OFF THE MAP

*Also by Pico Iyer*

The Lady and the Monk

Video Night in Kathmandu

THESE ARE BORZOI BOOKS
PUBLISHED IN NEW YORK
BY ALFRED A. KNOPF

# FALLING OFF
# THE MAP

*Some Lonely Places of the World*

## Pico Iyer

JONATHAN CAPE
LONDON

First published in United Kingdom 1993

1 3 5 7 9 10 8 6 4 2

© Pico Iyer 1993

Pico Iyer has asserted his right under
the Copyright, Designs and Patents Act 1988
to be identified as the author of this work

First published in the United Kingdom in 1993 by
Jonathan Cape
Random House, 20 Vauxhall Bridge Road, London SW1V 2SA

Random House Australia (Pty) Limited
20 Alfred Street, Milsons Point, Sydney,
New South Wales 2061, Australia

Random House New Zealand Limited
18 Poland Road, Glenfield,
Auckland 10, New Zealand

Random House South Africa (Pty) Limited
PO Box 337, Bergvlei, South Africa

Random House UK Limited Reg. No. 954009

A CIP catalogue record for this book
is available from the British Library

ISBN 0–224–03718–8

Printed and bound in Great Britain by
Mackays of Chatham PLC, Chatham, Kent

"This round gold is but the image of
the rounder globe, which, like a
magician's glass, to each and every
man in turn but mirrors back his own
mysterious self."

—MELVILLE

# Contents

## A Prefatory Note

Most of these essays were originally written, in somewhat different form, to introduce potential visitors to places of potential interest; to serve, that is, as open-eyed first impressions. In many cases, circumstances have overtaken me—Argentina has stabilized its peso, Cuba's destiny changes with every passing month, parts of Vietnam are probably unrecognizable. Still, I have not tried to update the chapters, or to allow myself the luxury of retrospective wisdom and prescience. These pieces were aimed to catch their subjects at interesting historical moments, but in moods that would not change with history's tides.

I would like to extend sincerest thanks to the editors who dreamed up or supported most of the journeys herein described: Harold Evans, Thomas Wallace, and colleagues at *Condé Nast Traveler*; Joan Tapper at *Islands*; Andrew Sullivan at *The New Republic*; and Henry Muller and friends at *Time*. Thank you, too, to the brothers at the Immaculate Heart Hermitage in Big Sur, for offering peace beyond measure and the perfect place in which to think about loneliness and space.

# FALLING OFF THE MAP

On every trip I took to Havana, the ritual was the same: I would get into a car with two of my friends (into a '56 De Soto most likely), and we would judder off towards José Martí International Airport. We drove past huge pictures of Che (BE LIKE HIM), past billboards that said SOCIALISM OR DEATH, THE MOTHERLAND BEFORE EVERYTHING, IT IS ALWAYS THE 26TH (of July, 1953), past long lines of women waiting for a bus. We spoke only in indefinite pronouns, so as not to arouse the driver's suspicions, pretending that we thought that everything was well, pretending that we did not hope to meet again. When we arrived at the airport, we would get out and sit under a tree just outside the battered terminal. There my friends would tell me about everything they planned to do as soon as they arrived in America: how they would open a bookstore, or take pictures of the clubs on Forty-second Street, or send all the jeans they could find back to their families at home. Then, when it came time for me to leave, they would turn and, without looking back, walk across the street to another tree and wait for a bus back into town. They couldn't bear, they said, to see me getting on the plane that they had been dreaming of for twenty-five, or twenty-seven, or thirty-one years.

That is one of the things that make me think of Cuba as a

Lonely Place. Just like the old men sitting on the terraces of the cheap hotels, showing you photos of long-lost fiancées ("Miss Dade County 1956"), or the trim government officials who ask, in perfect Eisenhower-era English, "Do they still play tetherball in the States?" Just like the statues of Don Quixote set on lonely hills across the countryside, and the pictures of Ava Gardner in the downtown restaurants; just like the tiny huddle of worshipers singing hymns on Easter Sunday, or the messages people give you to take to unheard-from mothers in the Bronx, distant cousins in Miami, an Indian—of course you can find him—by the name of Singh. Cuba is ninety miles from the United States, but it might as well be a universe away. Letters pass only infrequently between the two neighbors, and telephone calls are next to impossible (though it was once my mixed fortune to befriend, of all things, a telephone operator: every night in Havana, she would call me up, unbidden, and serenade me with Spanish love songs, and for months after I returned home, the phone would ring, at 2:00 a.m., 3:15 a.m., 4:36 a.m., and I would pick it up, to hear *"Oye, oye!"* and the opening strains of "Guantanamera"). Exiled from the Americas, deserted by its Communist friends, its only ally these days a xenophobic hermit state run by an octogenarian madman ("Querido compañero Kim Il Sung," run the greetings in the Cuban official newspaper, *Granma*), Cuba is increasingly, quite literally, a Lonely Place.

Lonely Places are the places that don't fit in; the places that have no seat at our international dinner tables; the places that fall between the cracks of our tidy acronyms (EEC and OPEC, OAS and NATO). Cuba is the island that no one thinks of as West Indian; Iceland is the one that isn't really part of Europe. Australia is the odd place out that no one knows whether to call an island or a continent; North Korea is the one that gives the lie to every generality about East Asian vitality and growth.

Lonely Places are the exceptions that prove every rule: they are ascetics, castaways, and secessionists; prisoners, anchorites, and solipsists. Some are famous for their monasteries (Bhutan and, in some respects, Iceland); some are famous for their criminals and cranks (North Korea and Paraguay). And though no one has ever formally grouped them together—save me—every Lonely Place conforms to the Paraguay described by its native writer Augusto Roa Bastos as "an island surrounded by land."

Yet loneliness cuts in both directions, and there are 101 kinds of solitude. There is the loneliness of the sociopath and the loneliness of the only child, the loneliness of the hermit and the loneliness of the widow. And as with people, so too with nations. Some are born to isolation, some have isolation thrust upon them. Each makes its own accommodation with wistfulness and eccentricity and simple, institutionalized standoffishness. Australia, a part of the Wild West set down in the middle of the East, hardly seems to notice, or to care, that it is a Lonely Place; Bhutan all but bases its identity upon its loneliness, and its refusal to be assimilated into India, or Tibet, or Nepal. Vietnam, at present, is a pretty girl with her face pressed up against the window of the dance hall, waiting to be invited in; Iceland is the mystic poet in the corner, with her mind on other things. Argentina longs to be part of the world it left and, in its absence, re-creates the place it feels should be its home; Paraguay simply slams the door and puts up a Do Not Disturb sign. Loneliness and solitude, remoteness and seclusion, are many worlds apart.

Yet all Lonely Places have something in common, if only the fact that all are marching to the beat of a different satellite drummer. And many are so far from the music of the world that they do not realize how distant they are. Both South Korea and North are zany, lonely places in their way: the difference is that North Korea is so cut off from the world that it does not know

5

how strange it is and cannot imagine anything except North Korea. This is how life is, I imagine North Koreans thinking: being woken up each morning with loudspeaker exhortations in the bedroom; being told exactly what clothes to wear and which route to take to work; being reminded each day that Kim Il Sung is revered around the world. In the half-unnatural state of solitary confinement, Lonely Places develop tics and manias and heresies. They pine, they brood, they molder. They gather dust and data, and keep their blinds drawn round the clock. In time, their loneliness makes them stranger, and their strangeness makes them lonelier. And before long, they have come to resemble the woman with a hundred cats in a house she's never cleaned, or the man who obsessively counts the names in the telephone book each night. They grow three-inch nails, and never wash, and talk with the artificial loudness of someone always talking to himself.

Burma, out of the blue, decides to call itself Myanmar and to name its most famous city, unintelligibly, Yangon. Iceland speaks a tongue that Grendel would have recognized. North Korea, which sees no tourists, is building the largest tourist hotel in the world, 105 stories high. And for many years now in Havana, across the street from the U.S. Interests Section, there has stood a huge billboard, with a caricature of a "Ggrrrr"-breathing Uncle Sam, next to the message SEÑOR IMPERIAL-ISTS! WE HAVE ABSOLUTELY NO FEAR OF YOU! There are more things on earth, Horatio, than are dreamt of in your philosophy.

When people think of Lonely Places, they tend to think of moody outcrops off the coast of Scotland, or washed-up atolls adrift in the Pacific. They may even think of the place where I am writing this, a silent hermitage above the sea along the unpeopled coast of northern California. But Lonely Places are not just isolated places, for loneliness is a state of mind. The hut where I am sitting now is utterly alone. For days on end, I do not hear a single voice; and from where I write, I cannot see a trace of human habitation. Yet in a deeper sense, the place is packed. I am companioned—by rabbits, stars, and wisps of cloud—in worlds far richer than any capital. The air is charged with presences, and every inch of hillside stirs. I watch for the skittering of a fox on my terrace, listen to the crickets chattering in the dusk, catch a blue jay's wings against the light. Birds sing throughout the day, and the ocean's colors shift. Everything is a jubilee of blue and gold, and at night, walking along the hills, I feel as if I am walking towards a starlit Temple of Apollo. A Lonely Place in principle, perhaps, but certainly not in spirit.

More than in space, then, it is in time that Lonely Places are often exiled, and it is their very remoteness from the present tense that gives them their air of haunted glamour. The door slams shut behind them, and they are alone with cobwebs and yellowed snapshots, scraps of old bread and framed photographs of themselves when young. The beauty (and pathos) of Burma today derives from the fact that it is stranded amidst decaying remnants of its former glory, and the poignancy of Cuba that in the midst of leafy university quadrangles, you will find bird-spotted tanks. You wind back the clock several decades when you visit a Lonely Place; and when you touch down, you half expect a cabin attendant to announce, "We have now landed in Lonely Place's Down-at-Heels Airport, where the local time is 1943 and the temperature is . . . frozen."

Yet Lonely Places are generally sure that their time is about to come. North Korea is just waiting for Stalinism to sweep the world and the Olympics to be held in the stadia it has built for them (the secret of his longevity, says Kim Il Sung, the world's longest-running dictator, is his optimism); Argentina is just waiting for the day when it will be a world power again, the cynosure of every distant eye. Lonely Places have seen Bulgaria, China, even Albania admitted, or awakened, to the world; they have seen the Falklands, Grenada, even Kuwait enjoy their moments in the spotlight. They tell themselves that even Japan was once a "double-bolted land," as Melville put it, and China, and Korea too; they tell themselves that tomorrow will bring yesterday once more.

Lonely Places are often poor places, because poverty breeds wonkiness and a greater ability to visualize than to realize dreams. Lonely Places are often small countries, because smallness gets forgotten: the tiny voices of Tibet, or Benin, or East Timor are seldom heard at international gatherings. But even huge countries can be Lonely Places, or have Lonely Places inside them, as anyone who has been to Siberia or Ladakh, Kashgar or Wyoming, can attest. Everywhere, in some lights, is a Lonely Place, just as everyone, at moments, is a solitary. Everyone sometimes dances madly when alone, or thumbs through secrets in a drawer. Everyone, at some times, is a continent of one.

Lonely Places are defined, in fact, by their relation to the things they miss. You would expect the western fjords of Iceland, or the depths of Tierra del Fuego, to be lonely; but there is a more unanswerable kind of loneliness, and restlessness, in Reykjavik and Buenos Aires, the loneliness of people just close enough to the world to see what they might be. Both American Samoa and Western Samoa are pretty little South Sea bubbles a world away from anywhere, and both are isolated hideaways lost in their own surf-soft universe. Both are graced by palm-fringed beaches, Technicolor cricket games, and huts echoing with cries of "Bingo" in the dark. But what makes American Samoa a Lonely Place is that it also has a zip code, a Radio Shack, and a Democratic caucus. It has American-style license plates, yellow school buses, and *Days of Our Lives*. It sends a congressman to Washington, but he is not allowed to vote.

Other Lonely Places are happy in their loneliness, or able, at least, to turn it to advantage. The Australians, it seems to me, thrive on their remoteness from the world and see it as a way of keeping up a code of "No worries, mate," while peddling their oddities to visitors: nonconformity is at once a fact of life for many, and a selling point. Others, like Tibetans, pine for a loneliness that is tantamount to peace. Still others have the bitterness of outcasts: if they cannot play the game, say the Libyans, why should you? "Ye Visions of the hills! And Souls of lonely places!" sang Wordsworth, who found all his solace and scripture in his loneliness, and saw in it purity and a return to buried-over divinity. Everyone is a Wordsworth in certain moods, and every traveler seeks out places that every traveler has missed. Everyone longs at times to get away from it all. Finding a sanctuary, a place apart from time, is not so different from finding a faith.

So it is that Lonely Places attract as many lonely people as they produce, and the loneliness we see in them is partly in ourselves. Romantic when first I visited Iceland, I found in it a province of romance; returning, four years later, in a darker mood, I saw in it only shades of winter dark. The Gobi Desert, for a couple in love, is as far from loneliness as Hong Kong, for a single traveler, may be close. Even a jam-packed football stadium may be lonely for the referee. It is common these days to hear that as the world shrinks, and as more and more places are pulled into the MTV and CNN circuit, loneliness itself may become extinct. Certainly, many Lonely Places—Vietnam and Cuba, for two—grow less remote with every joint-venture hotel, and cities like Toronto and Sydney, London and L.A., already seem part of some global Eurasamerican village, with a common language and video culture. Yet the very process of feverish cross-communication that is turning the world into a single polyglot multiculture is producing new kinds of Lonely

Places as fast as it eliminates the old. The lingua franca of parts of American Samoa is Mandarin, and Farsi is the second language of Beverly Hills. Japanese Joãos are returning to their grandfathers' homes from São Paulo as fast as German Hanses are taking Michikos back to Buenos Aires. Reykjavik is loneliest of all, I suspect, for the Thai girls who sit in the Siam Restaurant (on Skolavördustigur), alone with their mail order husbands. And even as the world contracts and isolation fades, half the countries around the globe are still off the map in some sense, out of sight, out of mind, out of time. There will never be a shortage of Lonely Places, any more than there will ever be of lonely people.

Lonely Places, then, are the places that are not on international wavelengths, do not know how to carry themselves, are lost when it comes to visitors. They are shy, defensive, curious places; places that do not know how they are supposed to behave. Yemen, Brunei, and Mali are Lonely Places; Paradise, Purgatory, and Hell are too. Desolation Isle is a Lonely Place, and Suriname, and California as seen by the Hmong. So, too, is the room next door.

## MY HOLIDAY WITH KIM IL SUNG

We were standing in front of the Tower of the Juche Idea, a 450-foot granite column, seventy tiers high, topped by a 60-foot torch, and symbolic of North Korean President Kim Il Sung's seminal notion of *Juche* (or self-reliance, as you and I and Emerson call it). "The Juche idea means that we should believe in our own strength, we are the masters of our destiny," my guide was telling me, choosing to ignore, for the moment, his country's patrons in Moscow and Beijing. "Even the South Koreans love our president Kim Il Sung," he continued, naming his country's most fervent enemies. "They know he is a great man." Around the base of the monument were "relievos" of the Kimilsungia flower, and a 50-foot-wide "hymn to President Kim Il Sung." At its foot were 230 congratulatory plaques, from Dar es Salaam, Finland, Zimbabwe, Lima, Gambia, and France. "Long live Kim Il Sungism!" offered the greetings from the New York Group for the Study of Kim Il Sungism.

It had seemed, at the time, a good idea, this holiday in Pyongyang. It was an unusual place, I suspected, somewhat off the tourist trail, stable (same leader for forty-five years), and quiet. It certainly had a distinctive culture—the tourist brochures featured "slogan-bearing trees" and offers of a thirty-seven day "Mud Treatment Tour"; the magazines talked of

movies like *The Report of No. 36* and *Order No. 027*, repro-
duced a painting by a ten-year-old prodigy (*An Athletic Meeting
of Crabs*), even extolled the possibilities for athletics ("Swinging
and seesawing are popular among women"). The North Korean
system of dance notation was, I had read, "recognized by the
art circle of the world as the most precious cultural treasure of
the contemporary times." And at one hundred dollars a day,
guide and driver and hotel and meals included, it was, according
to the *Condé Nast Traveler* Index, one of the cheapest vacation
spots in the world. Besides, the North Koreans were nothing if
not welcoming. "Golfers, come to Korea!" sang the pamphlets
in their embassy in Beijing. "Honeymoon in Korea." Even
"Animals and Plants Invite Tourists to Korea."

It had not, it was true, been easy to find the four-story brick
embassy. The guide in my Beijing hotel listed the twenty-five
most important foreign legations in the city, but its ally's was
not among them. No flag fluttered above the building's entrance, and no sign in English identified its allegiances.
Shrewdly, however, I deduced its identity from the fourteen
pictures of Kim Il Sung displayed on the billboard outside.
Inside, at eleven-thirty on a weekday morning, the embassy
had the feel of an evacuated palace: red-carpet staircases sweeping into emptiness, long, unlit corridors heavy with dust. Then
a round man appeared, speaking some English: "What do you
want?" I told him. "Ha! How long will you stay?" I told him.
"Ha! Where are you staying in Beijing?" I told him. "Ha!" That,
apparently, marked the end of immigration formalities; he gave
me a short form asking me to list "Mork undertaken," divested
me of five dollars (one can buy fourteen North Korean visas for
the same price as a single tourist visa to China), and told me to
come back the following week to collect a visa, a voucher, and
a ticket to paradise.

Chosonminhang Flight 162 from Beijing to Pyongyang was

not lavishly decorated; its only appurtenance was a brown paper bag in every seat pocket, saying "For your refuses." As soon as the plane took off, however, martial music struck up, the stewardesses began distributing bottles of Pyongyang Lager, and everyone was handed some in-flight reading. It was easy to spot the North Korean passengers: they were the ones with Kim Il Sung badges pinned to their hearts, who were ignoring the in-flight literature. It was easy to spot the Japanese business-men: they were the ones politely paging through a magazine that told them, "The heinous Japanese marauders will be forced out. And the star will be brighter over our land."

Such lyrical effusions apart, the magazine gave a very clear account of the land we were going to visit. It included pictures of machines and generator rooms, quotes from the Great Leader (helpfully printed in bold type), and—more promising still—photographs of a "Happiness-Filled Pleasure Park" ("Mad mouse makes you rhythmical and buoyant," advised the cap-tion). It told of a film director's agony as he realized that "my literary inspiration and spirit, knowledge and power of the pen seemed to be too poor or weak to represent the greatness of Comrade Kim Il Sung." Frankly, I could understand his prob-lem: the Great Leader was a "great comrade, great man and fighter," I read on one page, "a great thinker, politician and strategist . . . a great man and father of the people."

Self-possession, I gathered, was never easy in his company. "I was attracted by benevolent President Kim Il Sung with a bright smile," wrote a glamorous Hong Kong actress who had sung "A Whistle" before the North Korean president. "He seemed to smile all the time looking at me. When I sang the third stanza he looked at the stage . . . through binoculars with a smile." Soon the tension was getting unbearable. "I was so excited that I nearly fell to the stage."

I mopped my brow and put the magazine down.

The minute we landed at Pyongyang International, seats began crashing down on legs and suitcases on heads. We were led into a bus to take us to the terminal, and the martial music started up again. Inside, a few lipsticked soldiers apprehended me as soon as they saw me walking around alone. Then a tall, debonair young man, with a nonchalant Left Bank air, puffing on an Albanian cigarette, came up and extended a hand. "I am your guide," he began smoothly, ushering me into a white Volvo sedan. "What is your occupation? What is your religion? Have you been to South Korea? What were you doing before you came to China? What will you do after you leave China?" We drove through the sepulchral dusk, rows of featureless concrete towers looming through the gray on every side, the gloom relieved only by an occasional *Sound of Music* billboard. His conversation exhausted, the guide confiscated my passport and scowled. We passed more paintings of workers singing at the heavens. "Korean and Chinese are faintly similar?" I tried. "Totally different," he replied.

At the Pyongyang Koryo Hotel, which is forty-five stories high, I was led into an elevator that was as naked as an interrogation chamber, save for some overhead klicg lights. Then I was taken to my "Deluxe Room." This was a four-room suite, almost entirely bare—one of its chambers was naked even of a trash can. The refrigerator next to the wall was likewise empty. The hotel was rich, however, in mirrors: there were mirrors in every passageway, huge four-sided pillars of mirrors in the lobby, ninety-four mirrors in the hangarlike drawing room. It was a curious place, but comfortable: there was a calendar on the wall, featuring four important dates in the life of Kim Il Sung; there was a black-and-white TV, on which children could be seen reciting slogans; and though there was no lock on my door, it was graced by a five-digit number.

"It's going to be a long three weeks," a U.N. official was

saying as I went into the dining room for dinner. "Today they took me to the Botanical Garden and showed me all the plants named after Kim Il Sung, even all the bloody plants planted by Kim Il Sung." He had not, I gathered, seen Kimjongilia (named after the son of Kim). Like every closed country around the world, from Yemen to Bhutan, North Korea was teeming with these types—U.N. men and development aides, acronymed bigwigs and troubleshooters. Now they were seated in the dining room, German and Chilean and African, many in their most formal gear, surrounded by ninety-four reflections of themselves and picking at some grizzled rainbow trout. Around me, a familiar chorus rose up. "They're very nice, these people, but totally hopeless." "Their problem is they're overenthusiastic. But you can't tell them that, of course, and . . ." I, for my part, recalled the counsel of the in-flight magazine. "If you talk in the daytime, you'll be overheard by a bird," it had advised. "And at night by a rat."

Later I decided to take a walk around Pyongyang. It was an unusual place, just the same as in the photographs: there were no cars or bicycles along the streets; almost no shops or restaurants or cinemas; nothing, in fact, to distract from the spotless and unworldly hush. I walked for two hours round the city, but I came across no shocks or surprises, nothing charming or touching or strange; nothing at all, in fact. There were no smiles on the people's faces, no fears, no expression. The ashen pallor of a ghost hung over the huge, unbending, carless streets. Here, in a sense, was Marxism in the raw and by the book; both the apotheosis of the system and its epitaph. The block-capital streets and numbered towers, the two-hundred-foot monuments and impersonal megaliths, the featureless statues and murals, seemed a kind of abstract of Communism, as flawless as a blueprint; they also seemed a kind of memento mori, the last souvenirs of a system that was elsewhere all but extinct.

The more modern the buildings in Korea, the more the country felt outdated. Korea, in that sense, was generic.

And as in no other Communist country I had seen, there seemed no chinks in the wall here, no murmurs of dissent or whispers of "Change money?"; no curious glances in the street; none of the hustlers and hookers who are the main appointments of every state-run hotel. Nothing, in fact, to smudge the place or make it distinctive. Everything was just the way Kim planned it, executed with unswerving efficiency. The first time I tried to walk across one of the deserted avenues, I was instantly sent back by a red-flare-waving policewoman.

Then, however, I came upon my first surprise: in a huge and half-lit square, two hundred people had gathered, late on this Saturday night, in concentric circles, tidily arranged behind a leader. Silently, solemnly, they began walking through a series of military-style dances, the steps of their ghostly pantomime echoing through the night.

The next day, my sightseeing began in earnest. I was taken to the Grand People's Study House (with a "capacity of containing 30 million volumes"), the 150,000-seat stadium built for the 1988 Olympics, the 180-foot Arch of Triumph ("For its ideological content, size, architectural style and the representation of sculpture," the *Korea Guidebook* had explained, "the Arch of Triumph attains the highest perfection of monumental art"). "It's amazing it's so much like the Arc de Triomphe!" I marveled. "Totally different," snapped my guide.

Later, standing in the shadow of the seventy-foot bronze statue of the "peerless patriot and national hero," he extended a sweeping arm across the whole Orwellian skyline. "At first," he explained, "we did not know how to make buildings and sculptures. We tried, but it was not beautiful. But we tried and tried again. Now look." I mumbled something about the economic costs of such monumentalism. He looked incredulous. "How can you say our economy is weak when we have all this?" Kim Il Sung had built up the whole nation out of the rubble of war; having begun with a tabula rasa, he had enjoyed the rare opportunity to construct an entire nation in his image, stamped over with his monogram. Now, my guide went on, fifty thousand new flats were going to be completed in honor of the "sun of the nation's" eightieth birthday in 1992. It fell, appropriately enough, on Income Tax Day. That might also be the occasion when he handed over power to his son, Dear Comrade Kim Jong Il (or One Right Way Kim, as my guide translated). "Enemy propagandists say that this is a family dynasty," he explained. "But we need a leader just like Kim Il Sung. Who better than his son?"

Occasionally, as we drove, we saw people, always in groups, marching in regimental ranks to work, to the sound of exhortatory loudspeakers, or gathered in long lines at bus stops. By nine-thirty on this Sunday morning, enormous color-coordinated crowds were already practicing "mass card games" in Kim Il Sung Stadium (the Koreans are world champions of "mass games"; they have "mass games" majors in college and practice card patterns every day in school). The enormous expanse of Kim Il Sung Square was filled with children standing in the rain, "dancing hand in hand to the tune of the light melodies of 'Pyongyang Shining under the Rays of the Lodestar.' " Everywhere I looked, people were filing along in groups, two by two, in Indian file, with a leader at their head, like kindergartners on a field trip. "People are the most valuable thing in the world," my guide informed me, making them sound like subway tokens.

Making contact with these valuable things, however, was no easy matter. For though every child who passed me in the street gave me a "Welcome" salute, and though certain citizens had been designated to wave to foreigners, conversation did not seem imminent. For one thing, the hotel was sequestered in the western suburbs, within walking distance of almost nothing; for another, no taxis were available, and foreigners were not allowed to carry Korean money. This was a little disappointing. "Visitors are bound to make many friends in Korea," the brochures had promised, going on to point out, "There are no extremes of hot or cold" (the average temperature in January, it explained, was −8° Celsius).

For lunch, the two of us went for a banquet at a traditional Korean-style restaurant. Again our room was utterly bare, even of paintings or scrolls. The brochures, I remembered wistfully, had promised a chafing dish, gray mullet soup, and viper wines. Afterwards, I was taken to the humble thatched cottage at Mangyongdae, or "All Seeing Hill," where the "all-triumphant, resolute and incomparable leader" had spent his childhood, "nursing his great revolutionary will." I had already—in my first few hours in the country—seen his first wife's tomb, his uncle's grave, his cousin's headstone. Now I was able to enjoy his grandmother's broken kimchi jar and his great-grandfather's tiny study (though here there was some ambiguity: was it his *great* grandfather, as in "great man and father of the people," or merely his great-grandfather?). Hundreds of devotees lined up in the drizzle to have their pictures taken in the cradle of the revolution as hymnlike organ music was piped in through the extravagantly landscaped grounds; my guide pointed out the "many beautiful trees and marvelous pebbles contributed by the people." In the bushes, scores of workers labored silently to keep the gardens perfect.

"Our leader began his Communist struggle in 1925," the guide told me.

"But he was only thirteen then!"

My guide nodded sagely.

Nearby was the famous Mangyongdae Fun Fair, built to "cater for over 100,000 visitors a day." On this day, however, I counted fifteen, or roughly three for every functioning ride. I began to fear that mad mouse might not make me rhythmical and buoyant.

"Did your president come here?"

"Oh, yes," said the guide, his face flushed with the seemingly genuine joy he reserved for such moments. "And he was surrounded by hundreds of children."

It was silly of me to have asked, I suppose: soon enough I was seeing the plaque commemorating his visit to the video arcade (reverberant now with the sound of toy guns). Within twenty-four hours, I was being shown the hugely blown-up color photographs of his Fun Fair trip. The "eminent Marxist-Leninist and outstanding military strategist" had chosen the Fun Fair site himself, I read in a book called *An Earthly Paradise for the People;* and in the book *The Great Man Kim Jong Il,* I learned that the younger Kim had personally demanded that a Jet Coaster be made 1,500 meters long. The Jet Coaster, he had remarked, "is very good for developing boldness in young people."

By now, things were beginning to fall into a pattern.

"What is that statue?" I asked as we drove past a series of *tableaux vivants* and four-hundred-foot Korean monuments to Korea.

"Oh, Juche," said my guide, almost casually.

The Juche idea was, of course, much on my mind as the days went on. Luckily, I had many opportunities to explore it further. The main headline in the *Pyongyang Times* was "A letter to President Kim Il Sung." Page 2 featured a report on a meeting of the Asian Regional Institute of the Juche Idea (ARIJI); page 3, by good fortune, featured another report on the meeting of the Asian Regional Institute of the Juche Idea. In my hotel bookstore's display case, there were 114 different works, all of them by Kim *père* and *fils*, in Japanese and Arabic and everything in between; behind them were fourteen more shelves, double-stacked with other titles whose genres were usefully specified—*Immortal History: Revolutionary Aurora* ("A Cycle of Novels"), *The Mother of Korea* ("A Biographical Novel"). I saw two books that did not seem strictly relevant: *Story of a Hedgehog* and *Boys Wipe Out Bandits*. But all the rest, thank Kim, stuck assiduously to the main theme: the Great Leader's brief biography stretched across 1,808 pages.

I also took the opportunity, while here, of purchasing a copy of Kim Jong Il's ground-breaking study, *On the Art of the Cinema*. In it, the Dear Leader begins, surprisingly, by contending that "Art and Life are important activities." He goes on to pronounce that "Make-up is a noble art." He concludes, with typical boldness, by asserting that "A person with a low level of technical skill cannot make an excellent technician."

People say that Pyongyang is a dreary city, but I found no shortage of diversions there: I was taken to the subway stations (with their 250-foot mosaics, marble pillars, and gold chandeliers, built at air-raid-shelter level), and to the Thermal Power Station; to the Korean Revolutionary Museum, and to a performance by the Korean People's Army Circus (whose artists wielded guns while doing handstands and chanted slogans while revolving in midair). I even got a tour around the five-hundred room Children's Palace. "Children are very important," my guide pointed out. "We must always think of the future." The future and the past, in fact, seemed the places where the North Koreans felt most comfortable: anywhere but now.

"The system is like a big family," he went on.

"Does your president remain close to his family?"

"Yes," he said. "But Kim Jong Il has his own room. He is grown up enough. He is forty-eight."

The deliriously smiling infants at the palace were kind enough to put on an hour-long variety show just for foreign guests. In one dance, a laid-back cicada, cradling a guitar, tried to persuade a group of smiling ants to join him in the shade. The hardworking insects, collective-minded to the end, smilingly rebuffed him, and when a blizzard came, the cicada was left friendless and unprepared. "This is a simple parable," my guide whispered to me. "But it has a big meaning. For example, if we try at a socialist revolution . . ."

There was also much else to do. At night, in Pyongyang's equivalent of the Rainbow Room, I heard a six-piece band play "The Isle of Capri," and I once played billiards with a large Bavarian businessman made maudlin and drunk by the fact that the North Koreans had unexpectedly agreed to pay off a fifteen-year-old debt to his company. Downstairs, in the blue-lit Koryo Tea Room, the Village People were once again in fashion. I was pleasantly surprised to read that in the Second Pyongyang Film Festival, the Gold Torch for documentaries had been given to a Korean film; the Koreans had also taken the gold in the women's adult group and the junior group events of the World Radio Finding Championships (and a silver in the junior group individual event). They had ample occasion to practice, I imagined: every radio in the country, after all, was fixed so as to receive only one acceptable frequency.

And so great was the triumph of nurture over nature here— or of mind over matter—that the North Koreans looked, to my eye, quite different from their cousins and brothers in the south; in some respects, indeed, their ways seemed more refined—or beaten down—than the pell-mell boisterousness of Seoul. Yet in many ways, it was easy to see how the militaristic drills, the pragmatism, the collective-mindedness of the North Koreans, their tireless construction of concrete towers and fanatical determination to make good—no pain, no gain!—were not so differ-

ent from what one found in the south. In that sense, North
Korea, for all its anonymity—its air of Everyplace—did seem
a distinctly East Asian place. For all across the region—in Japan
and South Korea as much as in China and North Korea—one
finds the same remarkable gift for regimentation and self-sur-
render, for hard work and discipline, as if the religious impulse
had simply been channeled toward country or company or
cause. It hardly seemed to matter whether the object of this
devotion was nominally capitalist or communist. And it was
scarcely a surprise that these proudest and most standoffish of
countries were also famous for their nationalism and xenophobia
(the "Hermit Kingdom" tag has been passed around from one
East Asian country to the next for centuries). Certainly, a pro-
fessedly "homogeneous nation," which boldly asserts that it has
"never had mixed blood with other races," and a country where
50 percent of the people, by one estimate, have the same surname (Kim)—"The characteristically photogenic face is a typically Korean face," wrote the cineast Kim Jong Il—has a head
start when it comes to single-mindedness and solidarity. My
guide, in fact, took pains to stress patriotism far more than
Marxism; his country, he implied, was the lodestar of his love.
And "the people who do not have a patriotic idea," he said, in
a rare burst of fury, "they are no better than animals!"

My guide—an uncommonly urbane character, articulate,
quick-witted, and fluent in Urdu—had seen the world outside
North Korea during three years of study in Pakistan. But he
had seen the world through North Korean eyes, and he could
not help but feel that, by comparison with the poverty and chaos
of other parts of Asia, his was an unusually civilized country. He
accepted that his land was not perfect and conceded that there
might be dissidents; but peer pressure was so great, he said,
that the few were bound to get swept along by the many. (Once,
he explained, when he was tapping his cigarette in the street,

his seven-year-old son had quickly challenged him: "Father, why do you do this? My teacher says you should use an ashtray!") His greatest strength, indeed—the result, perhaps, of much practice—was in making preemptive strikes, countering my criticisms before I had even made them. "We are not a rich country," he conceded. "But we have pride. All this we have achieved by ourselves." Westerners, he went on, "say we do not have freedom. But we have a different concept of freedom." His government, he explained unexpectedly, deliberately made Pyongyang gray so that not too many people would move there.

The only thing that upset him was the fact that some countries were not strong enough for Communism. "In other socialist countries," he said, "it is not real socialism. The young people, they have stupid ideas." When I asked him whether his people were worried at all by the worldwide repudiation of Marx, he sounded adamant. "A strong country does not worry about the world situation. A terrier cannot harm a strong person." His confidence struck me, in fact, as genuinely unshakable. "When you go home," he pleaded, "don't repeat my propaganda. Just tell your friends what you saw and thought and felt here." He really did assume, I think, that seeing was believing here; that to know North Korea was to love it. He could not imagine that anyone could lay eyes on the modern blocks and enormous statues of Pyongyang and not want to commit himself to this socialist paradise.

My last day in Pyongyang, I decided to try one last time to walk across the deserted street. As soon as I reached the other side, however, I found an angry citizen waiting to reproach me. The next time I found an empty road I wanted to cross, I, like everyone else in Pyongyang, descended into one of the unlit, but luxurious, underground passageways, joining the ranks of expressionless faces.

"Welcome to Jujuy! Jujuy is the capital of the province of Jujuy!" cried the perky tour guide, a Joel Grey look-alike, as our "Bridge of the Incas" minivan bumped across the darkened plains of the Andes. "We are now in the province of Jujuy. The capital of Jujuy is Jujuy!" This pronouncement, unremarkable at the best of times, was not made easier by the fact that "Hoo-hooee" sounds as if it consists of nothing but vowels.

"Un *Arabe*," whispered a Frenchman called Yorick (alas, poor man, I knew him well). "That is why he is so slow. You must never forget history! The Arabs lived in Spain for seven hundred years!"

"This is Jujuy," the guide went on, undeterred, as we drove past the inevitable Korean department store, the lottery shops, the esoteric bookstore. "Jujuy is the capital of the province of Jujuy!" We stopped in a desolate Indian village, narrow, deserted alleyways running up to craggy red-rock canyons. A Belgian got out and took a video of his meat. A local boy recited a poem about his misery, and three large Argentines at the next table wept over their beef. The Frenchman and I went back to discussing which was the dirtiest race in Europe, he arguing passionately for the English, and I, *hélas*, for the French.

Then the van started up again, and the guide returned to

outlining the relationship between Jujuy and the province of Jujuy, in French, Spanish, and English, none of which could be told apart. "I am a sightseeing guide, not a homosexual guide," he volunteered unexpectedly. A lonely gaucho, with a weathered Indian face, plodded slowly on his horse across the empty pampa; a boy walked past carrying a wriggling iguana by the tail, home to his mother's cooking pot. The guide took a break from his exertions just long enough to quiz me on the immigration policies of the U.S. and to confess a lifelong urge to migrate to Australia. He was twenty-two, he added disarmingly, and he had been in this business eight years. The Frenchman muttered something venomous about the absence of free-market competition in the tour-guide trade.

After fourteen hours of this—we had set out that morning at five forty-five—I began to feel that I knew Jujuy fairly well, and was all too glad to tumble out of the van back into my hotel. But later that night, when I went to the local casino (not far from the bingo hall and just down the street from the office where they were announcing lottery winners), I suddenly heard an all-too-familiar voice behind me. "Good morning," it piped (it was 10:30 p.m.). I turned around to see the frisky young guide adjusting a bow tie above his tuxedo. "Jujuy is the capital of the province of Jujuy," I reminded him. He looked exultant "Tomorrow you go to Cafayate?" "Yes." "We meet at six forty-five! I am your guide! Good morning!" Preparing himself now for a moonlighting spell as a croupier, the poor man was apparently going to be working for thirty-six hours without stop.

The chaos and commotion of the day were not, it is true, very typical of Argentina, a nation that carries itself with the fastidious dignity of a maître d' anxious to assert his distance from all riffraff. But the episode did bring home to me that *la situación* (as the Argentines call their economic crisis—inflation was recently projected at more than four million percent a year) exists on more than paper. It reminded me that the friendly restraint of the people is maintained at some considerable cost. And it proved that, for all the partying till dawn and black-tie revelry I had seen across the country, it really was true that many Argentines were being forced to take on two, or even three, jobs to survive.

All that had been easy to forget amidst the fifth-arrondisse-ment comforts of Buenos Aires, a city more fashionable and deluxe than anything I had seen in Paris or Milan. In the relent-lessly chic quarter of Recoleta, I had felt closer to Belgravia than Bolivia as gilt-edged society ladies showed me their pictures in recent editions of *Town & Country* and boys in leather jackets committed Margaret Thatcher to hell. I had ended up, so it felt, in some extravagantly translated version of Europe—its elegance made more absolute by its distance from its source—where grandes dames in Impressionist-filled apartments told me of shooting parties with the Duke of So-and-soshire and how "simply mahvelous" were the penguins of Patagonia; while tycoons dropped the name of "Jackie" (the Maharaja of Baroda) and deplored the growing "commonness" of Monte Carlo. When I tried to put the two scenes together—the pressures of hyperinflation and the designer assurance of the beau monde—the only thing I felt I could be sure of was that Jujuy was the capital of the province of Jujuy.

Argentina is one of the longest countries in the world, stretching from the subtropical jungles of Brazil to the frozen wastes of Antarctica, a country almost as large as India, with only a sixth as many people as Indonesia has; yet on our mental map, at least, it is a Lonely Place. Colombia, we know, means drugs; Peru means Incan ruins; Brazil means fun. But what do we know of Argentina? We may hold a few darkly romantic images of the place—of gauchos and the tango, Sabatini and Borges, repressive military juntas and dashing polo players—but few of us realize that it is a country large enough to contain all contrarieties. A vast, rich immigrants' hope that has always been seen as a land of opportunity, Argentina sounds in the guidebooks like a United States of (South) America, a southern reflection of our home. It has, after all, a soigné, highly sophisticated city in the east; cowboys in the high sierras of the west; in the center, great plains and commercial centers; to the northeast, famously romantic waterfalls; and, amidst the baronial ranches of the south, oddity and a kind of Flannery O'Connor isolation. Yet to liken it to the United States is not to do Argentina justice. For Buenos Aires has a kind of café society cosmopolitanism that could put New York to shame. The mountains in the west have foothills taller than the Rockies. The Iguazú Falls are twice the width of Niagara; and the sprawling *estancias*, or ranches, are in some cases larger than whole countries. As for the unending wasteland of the Patagonian plains, blurring into the chill extremities of Tierra del Fuego, it is the last word in strangeness, all but synonymous with the ends of the earth.

Most of all, though, what makes Argentina a Lonely Place— and something quite other than its ostensible twin—is its longing, in the midst of New World spaces, for the Old World it has left. And that curious kind of displacement, played out in Wild West châteaus, finds its truest reflection, ultimately, in the madness of a roller-coaster economy that makes the country a bargain one season and an extravagance the next: to cite but one example, a visitor who changed his dollars into australes five years ago would now have to pay $100,000 for a taxi into town. A night in a good hotel would cost him roughly a million dollars.

The first, and probably the last, cliché you'll always hear about Argentina is that it's European, and certainly its international

27

debts are never surreptitious. The Claridge Hotel is just around the corner from Harrods department store, and the clock tower in the Plaza Británica is modeled, down to its chime, on Big Ben; the gray Peugeots sitting along elegant, tree-lined boulevards in the rain could almost belong to professors at the Sorbonne. When they were constructing "the Paris of the Americas" in the nineteenth century, Buenos Aires's developers shipped over huge statues, cobblestones, even whole buildings from Europe; and to this day, six in every seven Argentines claim direct European descendancy (more Italian, as it happens, than Spanish). There are virtually no blacks in Argentina, and very few Indians; in the cities' trendiest cafés, the dominant color is blond.

But things are a little more quirky than that. For Argentina is also rich with Basques and Welsh, and has a Jewish community of 250,000. Tens of thousands of Koreans live here now. President Carlos Saúl Menem is, famously, of Syrian descent. And one day, as he threaded his way through rush-hour traffic, a Saudi Arabian cabbie gave me a thirty-minute introduction to Mormonism. Everyone is hyphenated here, and the melting pot has been nothing if not vigorously stirred: the first time I opened up the *Buenos Aires Herald,* I found a picture of a schoolteacher at "St. Paul's College, Hurlingham," with the inimitable, and thoroughly Argentine, name of Margarita Churchill Browne de Gómez. At its best, Argentina can seem almost like an anthology of greatest hits: Parisian streets, Milanese styles, and Knightsbridge manners; American spaces, Continental cinemas, and Oriental bazaars.

As I settled down in my hotel along the gracious streets of Recoleta, however, the place I felt closest to was the Upper East Side of New York. Bejeweled matrons led their pedigreed dogs past Charles Jourdan and Guy La Roche, and private-school kids shuffled home in blue blazers and tartan skirts.

Riding-school girls with Benetton bags buzzed up to ninth-floor gold-paneled apartments, and eight-year-old boys strode along with rolled-up umbrellas—all of them graced with the thoroughbred, golden-skinned confidence of future dance-school graduates. The nearest disco was called Snob, and a shop down the street was Connoisseur Snob. Buenos Aires, in fact, was the first place I'd ever visited where I always felt underdressed: when I went to a tearoom, my first afternoon in town, at three o'clock on a weekday, every single male in the place—but me— was wearing a tie. Only a few years before, men had been arrested for wearing shorts in the street.

After nightfall, the city's imposing sense of high style was even more overpowering. The first time I rang up a *porteño* (as natives of the capital are called), he invited me to meet him at his café around midnight. When I arrived, it was to find a long table of the country's *jeunesse dorée,* in cocktail dresses and tweed jackets, talking of Trastevere and CNN over bottles of champagne. "Life here isn't just comparable to life in Paris or New York," one of them told me, in fluent English. "It's better. Here I can live in a huge house for a hundred dollars a month. I can dine in four-star restaurants for ten dollars. Domestics are cheap too." Another explained that he was about to put his vintage American sports car up for sale. "Is there a market for that?" I asked. "There is a market"—he smiled charmingly— "for everything." When I asked him for an address, he pulled out a monogrammed gold fountain pen and scribbled it off with a flourish of antique elegance.

When finally I excused myself, at 2:30 a.m., all the partygoers looked decidedly surprised. Outside, the streets were so crowded I could hardly walk. I stopped by my local café, but every one of the thirty or so tables was taken. People buzzed around a kiosk selling the latest issue of *House & Garden* and *Mad.* The streets of Recoleta at 3:00 a.m., in fact, were like the

29

runway at some fashion show: one never-ending parade of long-legged, long-haired Dominique Sanda beauties, some of them dressed as nuns, some with stars on their foreheads, all done up in black leather microskirts and flawless makeup. I felt as if I were walking through the pages of Italian *Vogue*.

Meanwhile, every day, the economy was sputtering further towards collapse. Some of the money I received was printed only on one side; some had the denomination inscribed in ballpoint pen. Some was "provincial money," which was worthless as soon as you entered the next province. Interest rates had recently hit 600 percent a month; the new government had exhausted five economic programs in its first eight months; people were lining up all night outside the Spanish and Italian consulates. Argentina, the immigrant's dream, was becoming a land of would-be emigrants.

What was going on here? A roulette-wheel economy that had the quality of *opéra bouffe*; a *dolce vita* gaudier than anything I had ever seen before: I could not put the two together. One hint, perhaps, came from the observation of a British journalist, who, visiting Argentina eighty years ago, concluded that "Appearances count for everything." Another came from the description in the very English, and very sardonic, *Buenos Aires Herald* of the scene at the block-long Teatro Colón on Oscar night—akin, it said, to "a fancy dress ball on board the *Titanic*." Most ladies, remarked the paper tartly, "came dressed as wedding-cakes."

I got my best sense of Argentina's ruling paradoxes, though, when I left the well-coiffed streets of the Barrio Norte. For there is a Left Bank culture here, as well as a Right, and a world that falls beneath the scrutiny of either: the large red sign immediately above the Pierre Cardin store on Avenida Callao announces the COMMUNIST PARTY. And I felt I could better understand the constituency of Menem and Perón when I went into the rough, working-class district of La Boca. For it was here, in this broken-down, Neapolitan dockland area, that the blood-red graffiti on the walls read MENEM IS THE WORD FOR HOPE and EVITA GUIDES US, SAUL LEADS US, and it was here, in a blighted *West Side Story* neighborhood of broken-toothed laborers and secondhand guitars, that people looked to Diego Maradona or the Madonna for salvation (those streets not lined with ads for football schools were decorated with the sayings of Jesus). On one wall, outside a school, someone had scrawled, plaintively, "Today is not my day, but I live."

The most famous street in La Boca—and the tourist's reason for going there—is Caminito, a short alleyway of corrugated-iron houses painted as brilliantly as M&M's, yellow, orange, and green, and surrounded by an artists' showcase of murals, sculptures, and plaques. Walk around the back of the cheerful, party-colored houses, however, and you can see that the rainbow hues cover bleak and semibroken homes.

I got an even stronger sense of dispossession when I went one day to a soccer game just ten minutes away from the perfumed streets where professional dog walkers were doing their job. For as soon as I arrived at the game, I was surrounded by the other faces of the capital. Groups of young boys in torn shirts, with tangled shoulder-length hair, sat sullenly on stoops. An old woman with overbright yellow hair sold crosses. Six policemen on horseback paced up and down, and twenty-five riot police wielding staves stared back at their gun-toting leader. Every vendor who entered the place was thrown against a wall and frisked. And within the stadium compound itself—it seemed only apt—was a Justicialist Party office commemorated to Perón. Here, I thought, listening to the kids shouting *ché*, or buddy, to each other, were, quite literally, Evita's *descamisa-*

*dos*, or shirtless ones. In the stands, twelve-year-old urchins huddled around a joint; one of them wore a cap that said THE MILLIONAIRES.

Yet what was most remarkable to me at the game was not how rough it was but, rather, how sedate. As the fiercely partisan tattooed boys took their places in the stands, and the riot policemen took up their positions, and the boys began pogoing up and down, letting off cheap fireworks and scattering scraps of paper like confetti, I braced myself for an eruption of the rage and violence so common in Europe. But in this game at least, the supporters simply stayed where they were, jumping in place, calm in their way, and strangely well-behaved. Tidy matrons sat demurely in a section reserved for women, and senior citizens took up another section. Vendors sold cashews at grilles modeled on toy trains. Even the (English-language) team names here suggested a curiously antiquated, clubby kind of British world: Newell's Old Boys, Chaco For Ever, Racing Club.

This sense of self-possession was everywhere in Argentina: the sense of a people standing, very erectly, on imported ceremony. There were few beggars in the streets, or prostitutes, and almost everyone I met was honest (with the glaring exception of the taxi drivers in the capital, who seem bent on redressing the country's $60 billion foreign debt single-handedly). Twice in four days, people actually *refused* tips from me. And for all the bons vivants' round-the-clock haunting of cafés, the only unsteady things I saw in Argentina were the *palos borrachos*, or drunkard trees, that line Avenida 9 de Julio. This was a country where even the man banging an Andean drum in a folkloric show was a silver-haired CEO type in blue blazer, gray chinos, and tie.

Yet still, I felt, there was something buttoned up about the Argentine chic, and oddly homogeneous. And though everyone, especially in the capital, was beautifully and expensively dressed—the men like investment bankers, the women like Italian actresses—theirs was a strangely conservative, Brooks Brothers kind of elegance, the style, I thought, of a people not quite sure enough of themselves to take any chances. Here, in a sense, was high fashion by the book—even, perhaps, by the copybook. When I mentioned this to an Argentine friend, I was taken aback to find he agreed. "We are too much taken with British ways," this most beautifully mannered of hosts said to me. "With that whole notion of being a gentleman. We don't cultivate our own styles. That is why we are in danger of being colonial."

More generally, "the Argentine people of every class," as the nineteenth-century president D. F. Sarmiento observed, "have a high opinion of their national importance." And in a land distinguished mostly by its size, they seem determined to assert that bigger must be better. The Argentines boast that they have the widest boulevard in the world, in Avenida 9 de Julio, and the longest street in the world (if "street" is defined in certain ways), and, in the mud-brown Río de la Plata, the widest river in the world (though the Amazon, they concede, is wider in parts). Many of the hotels in Buenos Aires—and not even the four-star ones—call themselves "Grand." It is that somewhat peacocky kind of swagger that makes other Latin Americans as keen to dissociate themselves from Argentines as vice versa. "The Argentines consider themselves too good even for Europe," sniffed an American woman who lives in Rio. García Márquez put it even more succinctly: "The human ego is the little Argentine inside us all."

Argentina sets its aspirations so nakedly on display that it is never hard to find signs of pretension and absurdity. In the National Museum of Fine Arts, the first floor is all Rodin, Monet, and Degas; the second floor, astonishingly, features some accomplished, but utterly uninflected, Argentine copies of Monet and Degas, right down to pictures of twilight haystacks in Provence. The Alvear Palace Hotel in Recoleta boasts the almost smothering glass-and-gilt opulence of a mock Versailles; yet Paul McCartney Muzak is piping through its corridors. Even the zoo here is rich with replicas of the *Venus de Milo* and with animal houses that are done up like pagodas, columned Egyptian pavilions, and Russian Orthodox churches; but its tattered empty cages are taken over now by stray cats. It is this kind of grandiloquence that moved V. S. Naipaul, for one, to rage against the assumed sophistications of the place—and, even more, its belief that money can buy sophistication. Its air of civility, he wrote, in his devastating, if entirely unfeeling, essay "The Return of Eva Perón," was merely a cover for barbarism; Argentina was "a simple colonial society created in the most rapacious and decadent phase of imperialism."

Certainly, for my part, the longer I stayed in the capital, the more I began to feel that it was less like Europe than like some New Yorker's idea of Europe, a selective, sentimentalized, exile's version of a world that had faded long ago—Europe as it could be seen only at a distance of seven thousand miles. Much of Argentine life reminded me of the way that certain Indians speak English, preserving, in their Wodehousian cadences of "jolly good, old chap," an almost caricatured version of an England that exists nowhere but in the mind: homesick for a place that they have never seen. Argentina seemed, in some respects, more Old World than the Old; less *haute couture* than *hauteur couture*. It was almost a relief to see a girl in a T-shirt that said LIFESTYLES OF THE BROKE AND OBSCURE.

Much of this, of course, is part now of the standard image of Argentina, as a land of stylish melancholics sharing yesterdays. When Tyrone Slothrop in *Gravity's Rainbow* bumps into a crew of token Argentines, he quickly sees that for them "nostalgia is like seasickness: only the hope of dying from it is keeping them alive." Paul Theroux, too, sensed that the country's household gods were ghosts: "gloom was part of the Argentine temper . . . the hangdog melancholy immigrants feel on rainy afternoons far from home." Even the tango, the country's most salable commodity, plays off this air of brilliantined nostalgia: though it originated with poor men dancing together in whorehouses, it is now a repository of the country's glamorous image of itself, of saturnine rakes and black-dressed beauties. The ritual celebration of nostalgia is now itself part of the country's nostalgia for its vanished glories. (And even the tango has not gone untouched by the ironies of the class struggle—a few years back, after it became fashionable abroad, all the society ladies of the capital started taking tango lessons, eager to show off their expertise in this peasants' kind of sensualism.)

Yet the perennial sense of expectations unrealized is also what gives the country a haunting sense of poignancy. So much in Buenos Aires was built on a bombastic scale, fit for a city of kings; so much was erected to be worthy of a country named after a precious metal, its capital of Good Airs built on the River of Silver. The buildings that remain now are an admonition almost, a reminder of splendors that never quite materialized. The downtown tearooms, like the Richmond or the Ideal, were built on a heroic scale, rich with mirrors, fleurs-de-lis, and thick leather chairs; gray-haired old waiters still stand on a vanished dignity as they dish out boiled potatoes and pots of strong tea. But there is something increasingly dusty about these places now, and frayed—the architectural equivalents of those lonely, charming con men in Graham Greene who go around abroad in Old Etonian ties. The pathos grows more piquant when Argentines, translating their terms into English, speak never of "decay" but, always, "decadence."

This air of faded grandeur was strongest of all to me along

the Tigre Delta, amidst the cluster of islands, just twenty miles south of the capital, where the middle classes have traditionally kept their weekend homes. On the way to the resort, one passes gleaming stores thick with Maseratis, and sailing club after sailing club—160 of them in all. But on the day I visited, it was raining, and the area had a deserted hill-station poignancy. All resorts are sad out of season, of course, but this one had the lingering sadness of a world that was not sure its season would ever come again. I peered through the drizzle at the bright cottages and gabled summer homes, with their croquet lawns and tidy hedges. All of them looked empty now, and shuttered, their deck chairs pelted by the rain, their lawns overgrown with trees. Two children canoed with perfect form through the darkening afternoon. For Sale signs stood on landing docks, and a hand-painted wooden board, hard to read in the drizzle, asked QUIEN SABE? The determined cheerfulness of the names was almost heartbreaking—Tres Amigos, Capricho, Never Say Never—and the uninhabited cottages in the rain had all the mildewed pathos of an abandoned British suburb that had found itself, somehow, on the wrong side of the Atlantic.

"We Argentines are living a dream," an uncommonly thoughtful *porteño*, scion of one of the country's richest families, told me. "And a dream of an age that lasted only a second. A dream of an age that perhaps never existed at all. For a few years, between the wars, Argentines were the wealthiest people around—like the Japanese today, or the Arabs of fifteen years ago. They imported ice by ship. They took their cows on shopping trips to Paris. They bought anything they wanted. But this was only a very few Argentines. And later everyone wanted to share in that dream. At the end of the war, when Perón took over, there was sixty billion dollars in gold in the treasury." Perón, of course, deployed that money to create an enormous middle class and a standard of living that put Argentina closer than ever to Europe. With it, however, he created certain expectations of ease and comfort that have not always been realized, leaving a large middle class unable to live in the style to which it was accustomed, yet unwilling to relinquish its hopes.

And unwilling too—this *estancia*-owner continued—to work to make up the difference. "Argentines were used to making money very quickly. A railroad was laid down through an *estancia*, and overnight the owners of the *estancia* became millionaires. So people never had the idea of working for their money, as they do in the U.S. We're used to an easy life, and everything coming easily, and now we can't understand why things are different." In some sense, it seems, Argentina cannot forgive the rest of the world for surging ahead of it. And the desperate gaiety with which it keeps up the high life seems almost a sign of idle bravado. The economy is collapsing, yet most people I met seemed more interested in speculating than in earning money.

Speculations, though, come in many forms, and one of the distinct pleasures of Argentina for the visitor is that so many of its people can speak so eloquently and thoughtfully about their own predicament; everyone, in this most self-conscious of places, is an analyst—and, therefore, an elegist—of his motherland. That may help to explain why the country has always attracted as many travel writers as tourists—it is such a fascinating case study (and the one place I can think of on which Naipaul, Theroux, Chatwin, and Jan Morris have all written extensively). What makes the country so intriguing to the visitor, in fact, is precisely what can make it so agonizing to the resident: it has the urbanity to reflect on its steady loss of all that urbanity entails.

"This crisis is the best possible thing that could happen to Argentina," says an Anglo-Argentine, with a subversive gleam, as his friend, a novelist, buries his head in his hands. "It may at last bring Argentines down to earth. We've been living too long on dreams and expectations. And that's all they are— dreams and expectations!" Above us, the murals and frescoes of a cavernous hundred-year-old restaurant gather dust. The novelist, gloomily announcing that even democracy has been exhausted now, quotes Clemenceau's remark, on visiting Argentina, that this was a country with a wonderful future—and always would be.

Indeed, if conversation is one of the most stylish arts in Argentina, politics is one of the greatest sights; for the central issues of the day are played out in every street and café, in a land that seems almost to feed off soap-operatic calamity. The first time I went to the Plaza de Mayo, a group of old-age pensioners was holding up masks and waving banners outside the presidential Casa Rosada (now, all too fittingly, swathed in scaffolding). Nearby was a clamor of student nurses chanting, "We want teachers!" while under a nearby arcade, a line of haggard *peronistas* was staging some kind of hunger strike. The next day, the Mothers of the Plaza de Mayo conducted their weekly march, followed by a motley crew of complainants that included Trotskyites, Communists, and gays.

But the political pageant is hardly confined to the central square. The clangor of opinions is everywhere, as omnipresent as the mimes and clowns and illusionists who perform around the shopping streets. The Communist Youth are organizing a rally that somehow combines the fashionable issue of privatization with the fail-safe cry "The Malvinas [Falklands] belong to Argentina!" Outside the Greco-Roman Congress, under a lamppost consecrated to Thomas Edison, a Muslim is displaying

pamphlets that predict the advent of the Khomeiniite revolu
tion. On Calle Florida, the main pedestrian shopping street,
gaggles of old men conduct ritual debates ("This is an economic
problem!" "No, it is political!") in front of a wall plastered with
posters: one celebrating Menem; one outlining the rules for
buying and selling dollars; one showing a turbaned guru; and
the last pointing out that extraterrestrials are dispensing wisdom
directly to one Señora Valentina de Andrade.

Indeed, the fascination with flying saucers that so obsessed
the Argentine priest in Greene's *Travels with My Aunt* seems
almost a national trait. Wealthy denim matrons pore over ads
for parapsychology and devour the cover story of the Spanish
magazine *Muy Interesante*, with its "Manual for Living in Outer
Space" (another of its stories deals with "Transparent Bodies").
In remote Jujuy—the capital of the province of Jujuy—a Gnos-
tic group is offering a series of weekly lectures; in Mendoza,
the bookstores are heavy with Gurdjieff and Ouspensky. And
when I went to the annual book fair, an almost three-week-long
event that draws more than a million people, the flashiest sign
of all, advertised by a dazzling pink neon sign, belonged to the
Hare Krishnas (the stall next door was that of the University of
Moron). Menem himself took office on a day deemed astrologi-
cally propitious.

The other great rage in Argentina—which may respond to
the same kind of needs—is psychology. Freud and Lacan dominate the bookshop windows, and, as everyone always mentions,
there are three times more therapists and psychiatrists per
capita in Buenos Aires than in New York State. Streetside kiosks
sell magazines called "Real Problems in Psychoanalysis" and
others whose covers say, simply, "Anguish"; the hot issue
among the jet-setters is antidepressant drugs. What impressed
me most about Argentina was not just that shrinks are as com-

mon as occultists but that both, like health clubs, are the kind
of leisure-class accessory one usually associates with affluence.
And as affluence grows more precarious, the need for miracles
grows more intense. "We want even our politicians to be like
magicians," an Argentine told me, "just to wave a wand and
make our problems disappear."

Yet the problems, and the elegies, only mount as the country
gradually turns into one of those nations it has always looked
down upon. Not long ago, Argentina was the capital of Latin
American publishing (as recently as the forties, 80 percent of
all books in Spain came from Argentina); now Chile and Mexico
are taking its place. Of the country's three great modern writers,
Manuel Puig chose to live in Rio; Julio Cortázar lived (and died)
in France; and Borges spent much of his time on American
campuses, or, in his mind, in the company of Chesterton and
*Beowulf* (the fact that he does not seem Argentine may be the
most Argentine thing about him). On every side, the *belle
époque* seems to be receding fast. Yet in some sense, I could
not help but feel that unsettledness is almost native to the land.
More than 150 years ago, when Darwin came to Argentina, he
wryly noted that there had recently been fifteen three-year
governments in the space of nine months. And when Naipaul
visited eighteen years ago, the local currency was already deval-
uing by the day, and people were already searching for dollars
and taking on extra jobs. "I'd expect you to be confused here,"
a young local writer told me (she had studied English at summer
school in Eton). "Even we are confused. Because we keep
expecting things to change, but everything always stays the
same."

Through all this, however, the division between city and country remains as intense as during the bloody street fights of the
last century; and almost anything one says about the capital is

contradicted elsewhere. A few characteristics, inevitably, seem indigenous. When I arrived in the old colonial city of Salta, for example, the streets were still buzzing at ten-thirty on a weekday evening. Music blared out of an Arabic restaurant next to Maxim's. Just down the street from Benetton, a fancy bookstore showed off new copies of García Márquez, Kundera, *The Satanic Verses*—and *I Visited Ganymede: The Wonderful World of the Ovnis*, by Yosip Ibrahim. Shop-window girls swapped secrets in chic Italian cafés, and bulletins on windows offered "Yoga Classes for Children." In the main plaza, a couple of hundred striking architects were banging drums and waving banners and demanding "Real Social Justice." Nearby, in the cathedral, a poster of the Virgin Mary reassured, "Argentina: it is in crisis, but not in dissolution."

Yet apart from these common features, much of the country proceeds as if it has never been told that it is meant to resemble Europe. The great glories of Argentina, in fact, lie in its Nature. Wake up in the freshness of an early morning in Iguazú, and the forest glistens with a newborn clarity. Rainbows arc across the crashing falls, and blades of grass gleam emerald under dripping water. Toucans flood the trees, and fat lizards sunbathe amidst roots and branches. Later, as the day develops, coatimundis burrow and scurry across one's path, and serpents slither over catwalks. Above, far above, condors circle the blue with blackness. Though hundreds of miles from the Amazon, the area feels like a tropicolored Amazonian dream, the cover of some Latin American novel magically come to life.

And even for those, like Greene's CIA man, for whom the spread of 275 falls is "just a lot of water," the world around the falls feels Edenic. The greatest of all its wonders, for me, were the Nabokovian rainbows of butterflies—indigo, lavender, white, and gold—that skittered about my arms and alighted on my fingers till my fists were bright with yellow and black.

Turquoise jewelry on wings, glittering against the misting of the foam.

The other secret pleasure of Iguazú is that it allows one to slip across the border and, in the process, across centuries and continents. For Argentina and Brazil are as far apart as three-piece suit and one-piece thong; as fashion show and carnival; as Europe, in fact, and Africa. The Brazilians undress as routinely as the Argentines dress up. And the minute one arrives on the Brazilian side of Iguazú, colors brighten, buttons come undone, inhibitions slip away. Well-muscled boys in shorts preen and howl, flashing-eyed girls whisper in the husky seduction of Portuguese, the shops turn giddy with cartoony postcards setting off the falls with topless girls. Along the border, I could not help recalling what a wealthy Argentine administrator had told me, wistfully and with a touch of envy. "The Brazilians are a people of nature—simple people in paradise, like animals in the Garden of Eden. In Argentina, we live too much in our heads." Cross the border back into Argentina, and you feel as if you're reenacting the fall into self-consciousness.

Even better, Iguazú is a gateway into Paraguay. And though the inimitable General Stroessner is gone now, his notorious home for fugitives and deviants, where one car in every two is stolen and two-thirds of all goods are smuggled, is still its famous, irredeemable self. As soon as I stepped onto the sidewalk in Paraguay, a young boy offered me a packet of pink condoms. Another philanthropist blew the dust off a stack of pirated cassettes, including such classics as "Rod Steward: Greatest Hit's." Everywhere I looked, bored shopgirls were sitting over showcases heavy with pink panda-faced minipianos and Rambo .357 magnums. Casa Chen, Casa Mo Mo, Casa Very Good. At Casa Wang, the dusty cases were full of Bust-Emulsion creams and Cosmetic Pencil Sharpeners; at Casa Ping (just down from Casa Ting, and not so far from Casa Ming), boxes of Yu-fung Drop-Proof Multi-

Testers sat amidst forty-piece ratchet socket sets. Wild Arabic music flavored the air, and the smell of cheap foo yung. Taxi drivers played checkers with the rusty caps of soda bottles.

In the middle of the street sat stripped-down stolen Chevrolet Opalas and Ford Nopals, circled by policemen looking for bribes. A disembodied pair of stockinged legs jutted into the air. Casa Hokkaido, Casa Snoopy, Snoopy World. I saw UFO Beach Radios for sale ("sand resistant") and toucan-faced quartz watches. I saw an elephant that played the drums, three bears in caps, which mechanically skipped rope, a pair of roller skates shaped as elephants. I saw hamburgers clad in pink on skateboards, and telephones in the shape of penguins, sporting red bow ties. I saw gold-dealers and criminals and street-corner toughs. At the end of the day, Puerto Iguazú, back in Argentina, with its brassy posters advertising Brazilian *mulatta* girls and a Chinese show called Tra-Lá-Lá, seemed almost tame.

In the Andes, too, I found myself a universe away from the capital's feverish gaiety. It feels like siesta around the clock in the low, sunbaked villages of the northwest, with their long, empty streets and haunted shadows. Bowler-hatted women stand sleepy in the shade, selling ponchos and Batmobiles. Around them, the town stretches out like some forgotten settlement in New Mexico, white churches dazzling under high blue skies, cacti against hills as many-colored as an Indian quilt. In the dark, as Andean folk songs echo across the pampa, the place feels as lonely as the sound of panpipes.

Farther south, near the park-filled city of Mendoza (its willows and plane trees imported from Europe), the mountains are even more spectacular. In the silent, blue-sky villages, on a brilliant Sunday morning, bells toll parishioners to mass, and mountain light streams musky along avenues of elms. Nearby, a winding road slices through the snowcaps, past Incan ruins, all the way to the Chilean border. Yet even here, one is always in Argentina. "WARNING," announces the notice in a ski lodge. "It is prohibited here to speak of Politics; Economics; the Rise of the Dollar; the Cost of Living; Personal Finances; Unpaid Debts; Rising Costs; Various Anxieties. Be friendly; go easy on your Nerves."

It isn't always possible, of course, for locals to forget *la situación*—especially in places far from the sources of power. Even in dusty, pre-Hispanic villages like Humahuaca, the walls are scrawled with appeals for "Democracy Without Hunger." And even in Tierra del Fuego, there are busts of Evita. Even in Ushuaia, in fact, a drizzly, windblown settlement that calls itself the southernmost town in the world, shopkeepers confess their dreams of emigrating to Quebec two years from now, and un-wealthy squatters transport their houses, on sleds, along the main road.

Not surprisingly, perhaps, Ushuaia is pervaded by a polar stillness; and not surprisingly, perhaps, it looks like a mirror image of Isafjördhur or the other eerily silent Icelandic fishing towns around the Arctic Circle. The gray feels perpetual here, along the sludgy streets, and the town seems almost a study in gray—the water behind it like dishwater, the snowcaps above moody and looming, the sun a dull nickel in the sky.

Ushuaia is still an Argentine place, though, which means that it offers stylish art galleries and concerts of Ravel and the names of French perfumes above its row of duty-free stores. On a slippery gray outcrop in the silver light of the Beagle Channel, black cormorants line up like boys at a black-tie ball, while sea lions huddle on slick rocks in the steady rain, then bark and romp like dolphins in the freezing water. High up, near the glacier that overbroods the town, the snow is inches deep around the autumn auburn trees. And in the Museum at the End of the World, there are not only taxidermists' models of all the Fuegian birds, and skulls of three-ton sea elephants, but also, most excitingly of all, a copy of the famous Yahgan-English dictionary compiled by Thomas Bridges, the intrepid Anglican missionary who was the first foreigner to settle here (*okka*— "Oh dear me! Ah! Oh!" *okkonoma*—"To persist in asking for food, as a hungry child from his father"). In the same case is an even more touching symbol of the region's enduring strangeness: a copy of John's Gospel translated into Yahgan.

But the most magical of all Argentina's pleasures, for me, was Patagonia. The skies are celestial in this no-man's-land, lit up with unearthly shades I have never seen before. While driving through the desert, as a full moon set above the scrub, sending lavender and pink streaks across the sky, I could see nothing but miles of nothingness. Occasionally, an eagle circling above a carcass. A hut. The rusted shell of an abandoned car. A flock of ostriches. Around them all, stretching everywhere, miles and miles of nothingness.

Even the small towns in Patagonia are touched with a kind of Alice Springs desolation: the queer displacedness of boxlike settlements set down in a grid in the middle of nowhere. A town with the English name of Rawson is next to one with the Welsh name of Trelew and another with the Indian name of Guyman. But the town with the Indian name is, in fact, a cluster of Welsh red-brick cottages, with tidy rose gardens in the back and flowerpots lined up under white lace curtains. Red British postboxes stand on lanes called Miguel D. Jones and Juan C. Evans, and a central park remembers an idealized hedgerow-and-Spenser sceptered isle. Inside their little houses, Welsh women, speaking Spanish, serve traditional teas in semi-Wedgwood pots, with Cadbury's Milk Tray cups.

There are still eisteddfod singing contests in the pavilion in the plaza here (and an even truer sign of Britain—a kiosk flooded with reggae music, run by a polite skinhead with a John Lennon pendant around his neck). And as the shadows lengthen in the otherworldly light, shopkeepers sip their thick-bowled maté pipes, and boys play Ping-Pong in a tiny, one-room Adventist Temple. At night, the place is silent again, except in a couple of cafés where boys sit motionless with upturned faces, captive to Bruce Lee.

And then, of a sudden, one blustery autumn morning, I found myself alone in a colony of two million penguins, stretching out in crowds as far as I could see; thousands upon thousands of the engaging little creatures, shuffling backwards into their burrows, bending their heads together under bushes, scurrying along their "penguin highways." Down below, some of them were waddling into the clear blue water, preparing to travel north for the winter, while others padded off in pairs, like weary old men on their way to the pub. Around me, their plaintive, keening wails sounded like the cries of distant children in a playground. Yet as I walked among them, the quiet, cordial figures neither recoiled from me nor advanced, but simply stood there, heads tilted quizzically to the side, like professors waiting for another question.

That night, driving back across the flat Patagonian nothingness, flat as a map or a photograph, tango music playing on the radio in the dark, the ruddy-faced Welshmen with their sheepdogs behind me, the full moon turning the sea into a silver plate, and the penguins on their way to Rio for the winter, I thought back to the wealthy entrepreneur whom I had met in the capital, railing against Nixon's institution of the dollar standard. "Paper money's a fiction," he had almost shouted. "A fiction! It does not exist except in the mind. Soon there'll be some big changes in the world. You'll see! There'll be many, many surprises! And the leading powers are going to be the countries with the greatest resources—Australia, South Africa, Argentina!"

A little later, when I turned on the TV one Saturday night, it was to see President Menem on a variety show, smiling in a sea of blondes and crooning a song of his own composition. The next day, the government announced that inflation for the month was 95.5 percent.

*Cuba: 1987–1992*

## AN ELEGIAC CARNIVAL

> Gorgeous Cuba knows
> tornadoes that never swept
> tame northern lands.
>
> MELVILLE

Another cheerful day in Cuba. I wake up in the Hotel Pernik in Holguín and get into an elevator to go to breakfast. The elevator groans down a few feet, then stops. I press a button. The button falls off. I ring a bell. There is silence. I kick the door. The elevator groans up to the floor just left. Outside, I can hear excited cries. *"Mira!" "Dime!" "El jefe!"* A little later, the doors open, just a crack, and I see a bright-yellow head, and then a black face with a beard. "Don't worry," the face assures me. "You cannot move." The doors clang shut again, and I hear a crowd gathering outside, more "Psssts" and cries. Every now and then, the doors open up a few inches and a new face peers in to wave at me and smile. Then I hear a voice of authority, and as a chain gang of men strains to push open the doors, a teenager gets up on a stepladder and, methodically, starts to unscrew the whole contraption.

Twenty-five minutes later, I am released upon the Pernik dining room. My British guidebook, not generally bullish on things Cuban, waxes rhapsodic about the hotel's fare. "Eat and drink extremely well," it says. The Pernik, it adds, has "a long and appetising menu featuring steak in many forms, good fish and chicken, and fresh fruit and vegetables—even including avocado." Not today, it seems. "What would you like?" a smiling waitress asks. "What do you have?" "Nothing." "No eggs, no tea, no avocado?" "Nothing. Only beer." At the next table, a waitress is prizing open a bottle top with a spoon. The "typically cavernous Eastern European dining hall" is full of happy diners this morning, but not, it seems, of food.

Outside, my school friend Louis and I run into a woman from Aruba who is here to find her grandmother. The grandmother, unfortunately, is lost, but the Aruban has decided in the meantime to smuggle out a '56 Chevy. "Here the people have no salt, no sugar, only one piece of bread a day," she informs us as she gets into our car, "but this is a paradise compared with Aruba." Where are we from? England. "Ah," she sighs, "like Margaret Snatcher, the crime minister." Louis, a Thatcher devotee, accelerates. We drop her off at the airport and head for Santiago. Only four hours as the Nissan flies.

Driving along the one-lane roads, past sunlit fields of sugarcane, we pass billboards honoring the great revolutionary heroes (Martí, Guevara, O'Higgins), signs declaring SPEED IS THE ALLY OF DEATH, lonely ceiba trees, and goat-drawn carts. Flying Pigeon bicycles are everywhere, and vintage Plymouths, and hissing, rusted buses. Sometimes we stop to pick up hitchhikers, and Louis serenades them with passages from *The Waste Land*, ditties from the Grateful Dead, and—his latest attraction—manically pantomimed scenes from *The Jerk*. Bicycles, chickens, children swarm and swerve across the roads. I remember the time in Morocco when, on our way to the airport, he hit a dog. The dog bounded off unhindered; our Citroën limped to a halt.

Then, suddenly, out of nowhere, a bicycle swerves in front of us, there is a sickening thud, and our windshield shatters, splattering us with glass. I cannot bear to get out to see what has happened. But somehow, miraculously, the boy on the bicycle has been thrown out of the path of the car and gets up, only shaken.

A crowd forms, and, a few minutes later, a policeman appears.

"We're so sorry," I tell him. "If there's anything we can do . . ."

"No problem," he says, patting me on the shoulder. "Don't worry. These things happen. We're sorry if this has spoiled your holiday in Cuba."

Spoiled our holiday? We've almost spoiled the poor boy's life!

"Don't worry," he assures me with a smile. "There is just some paperwork. Then you can go on."

A car comes up, and two more imposing cops get out. They take some notes, then barrel up towards us. "These boys," says one. "No, no. It was entirely our fault." "These young boys," he goes on. "You will just have to fill out some forms, and then you can be on your way."

Soon we are taken to a hospital, where a young nurse hits me on the wrist. Then she asks me to extend my arms, to touch my nose, to touch my nose with my eyes closed. Luckily, it is a big target: I pass with flying colors.

Then we are taken to the local police station, a bare, pink-walled shack in the town's main plaza. Inside, a few locals are diligently observing a solitary sign which requests them to SPEAK IN A LOUD VOICE.

Across from us sits our hapless victim, next to a middle-aged man. Sizing up the situation, we go over to him. "Look, we can't apologize enough for what we did to your son. It was all our fault. If there is any . . ."

"No, no, my friends." He smiles. "Is nothing. Please enjoy your time in Cuba." Louis, overwhelmed, presents the family with a box of Dundee Shortbread, purchased, for just such occasions, at the Heathrow Duty-Free Lounge. A festive air breaks out.

Then we are ushered into an inner office. A black man motions me to sit before his desk and hand him my passport. "So, Señor Pico." "My surname, actually, is Iyer." "So your father's name is Pico." "No, my father's name is Iyer." "But here it says Iyer, Pico." "Yes. My family's name is Iyer." "So your mother's name is Pico." "No. My father's name is Iyer." "So your mother's name is . . ." This goes on for a while, and then a baby-faced cop with an Irish look comes in. He claps a hand on Louis's shoulder. Where are we from? England. "No wonder he looks like Margaret Thatcher," he exclaims, and there is more jollity all around. Then he leans forward again. "But you are from India, no?" Yes. "Then tell me something." His face is all earnest inquiry. "Rajiv Gandhi is the son of Indira Gandhi?" Yes. "And the grandson of the other Gandhi?" "No. He is the grandson of Nehru. No relation to the other Gandhi." "No relation, eh? Not a grandson of the other Gandhi?" The Irishman shakes his head in wonder, and the black man sits back to take this thunderbolt in. Then he resumes typing out his report six times over, without benefit of carbons.

Finally, he turns to Louis. "So your family name is Louis," he begins. "No, no," I break in, and add, "he cannot speak Spanish." There is a hasty consultation. Then the Irishman pads off, only to return a few minutes later with a trim, round-faced boss with glasses and a tie. "*Guten Tag*," cries the police chief, extending a hand toward me. "No, no," I say. "It's him." The police chief spins around. "*Guten Tag*," he cries, greeting Louis like a long-lost friend and proceeding to reminisce about a "*Freundin*" he once knew in Leipzig. Things are going swimmingly now. "Margaret Thatcher, very sexy woman!" exclaims the Irishman. "Rajiv Gandhi is not the grandson of the other Gandhi," explains the black man to a newcomer. "*Aber, diese Mädchen . . .*" the police chief reminisces. We could almost be at a Christmas dinner, so full of smiles and clapped shoulders is the room. "If this were anywhere else," Louis whispers, "if this were England, in fact, and a foreigner hit a local boy, they'd probably be lynching him by now."

At six o'clock—it is clear that the police plan to make a day of it—the police chief invites us to dinner at the town's only hotel. Guests of the police, he says. We sit down, and Louis spots a glass of beer. He orders one, and drinks it. Then another. Then another. The chief orders more beers all round, then proposes a toast to *Die Freundschaft*. The waitress drops off a few beers. "She worked in Czechoslovakia for four years," the chief proudly informs us. "How is the weather now in Prague?" Louis asks her in Czech. "I worked for four years in a Trabant factory," she answers. The police chief, exultant, proposes more toasts to *Die Freundschaft*.

"Paraguay is the only place in the world where you win at blackjack even if you're only even with the bank," offers Louis.

"*Gut, gut, sehr gut!*" cries the chief, more animated than ever.

We renew a few pledges to eternal friendship, then get up and return to the police station, which is sleepy now in the dark.

Louis sits down and promptly slumps over. A group of policemen gathers round him to peer at his handless watch.

Then, suddenly, he sits up. "I'm feeling really terrible," he announces and, lurching out to the terrace, proceeds to deposit some toasts to *Die Freundschaft* in the bushes.

The police chief, anxious, comes over. "I'm sorry," I explain. "We haven't eaten properly for a few days, we were somewhat dehydrated already, and he's probably anyway in a state of shock." With a look of infinite tenderness, the chief summons a lieutenant, and, one on either side of Louis, they take him to the hospital.

Ten minutes later, the team returns, all smiles.

"How are you feeling?"

"Great. All better now."

"Good."

Louis slumps over again, and I maintain our vigil for the man from the car rental firm who is due to take us to Santiago. He was expected at two-thirty. It is now nine-fifteen.

Suddenly, a policeman walks into the room and summons me urgently over. I hurry to his side. Maybe he will give us a lift? "You are an Indian?" he says.

"Yes."

"Then tell me something." He points to a TV. "Two months ago, we saw Rajiv Gandhi being burned. Why did they not put his body in the ground?"

What is the Spanish word for "cremation"? I wonder wildly. "*Cremación*," I try.

"Cremation, eh? Is that right? Thank you," he says, and walks out.

A little later, Louis gets up again and staggers to the terrace. More toasts to *Die Freundschaft* go down the drain.

"I'm really sick," he says. "I can't move. Just get me a bed."

I relay the request to the police chief.

For the first time all day, his commitment to our friendship seems to flag. "*Hier gibt es kein Bett!*" he barks. "*Das ist nicht Hotel! Das ist nicht Krankenhaus!*"

"*Jawohl, mein Herr*," I say, and we go on waiting for the car rental man.

Suddenly, headlights sweep into the plaza, and a car pulls up. I hurry outside. A man gets out, with an air of great briskness, and I hurry over to him. "So you are Indian?" he says.

"Yes." "Then tell me something, please. When Rajiv Gandhi died, why did they not put his body in the ground?"

"Cremation," I reply with tired fluency, and, satisfied, he gets in his car and drives away.

Watching this open-air university in action, the police chief is shamed, perhaps, by his earlier brusqueness. "Once," he tells me in German, "I traveled for six hours by train to Dresden to meet my roommate's sister."

"*Ach ja?*"

At 11:15 p.m., the car rental man appears, and we return to the inner office to do some paperwork. "So—your name is Pico?" "Well, my family name is Iyer." "So your father's name is Pico." "No . . ."

At 1:15 a.m., we pull up at last in front of the Casagranda Hotel in Santiago ("simultaneously dirty and suffocating," sings my guidebook), a famous old joint recently closed for fumigation, where we have a four-day reservation, paid for in advance in London. I leave Louis comatose in the back of our new car, sundry revelers singing and banging drums around him in the street. Inside the hotel, an enormous man is sitting next to a wooden cash register. When he sees my voucher, he looks unhappy. Party girls in backless dresses and well-coiffed boys stroll down the pitch-black staircase from the rooftop cabaret. A couple of them sit on a couch in the lobby and gaze expectantly in my direction. The enormous man looks desperate. I look worse. He picks up a telephone and starts dialing.

Thirty minutes later, he has found us alternative accommodations. At 2:15 a.m., a convoy of two cars, including one spokesman for the house of Gandhi, one new rental car and one immobile investment banker, pulls up at the Hotel Gaviota. As soon as it does, a young boy rushes out. "Welcome," he cries, in English. "How was your trip? Welcome to the Hotel Gaviota! It's great to see you!"

"Thanks."

"We have some Welcome Cocktails all ready for you! What will it be? A cuba libre? A daiquiri? Some *ron*? What would you like?"

"My friend cannot move."

"No problem. A Welcome Cocktail will help. It's on the house!"

"But he's already heard Margaret Thatcher impugned, almost killed a boy, and been taken to a hospital by a police chief speaking German."

"Sure!" says the boy. "That's why he needs a Welcome Cocktail. Please! My friends are waiting!" He points to the bar, where two young bloods are sitting hopefully in the dark.

I go over to Louis, now propped up in the lobby, and break the news to him.

He does not look overjoyed.

"The thing is, unless you order a Welcome Cocktail, I don't think you'll get a room."

"Okay, okay, just get me some mineral water." Realizing that this could entail a long wait—yesterday we had stopped in a small town to ask two boys for water and been told, "For water you must go to the next town! Only forty-five kilometers away!"—I go to the desk to do some paperwork. On one side is a sign that advises, CRAZY LOVE IS NOT TRUE LOVE. On the other, a stack of Cubatur brochures. "*Ven a vivir una tentación!*" Come to live out a temptation!

Proprieties observed, we follow our host on the ten-minute walk to our suites, made-for-mobster caverns from the fifties, with mirrors all round, and enormous makeup areas for showgirls.

"This is okay?" the young boy asks.

"Sure," I say. But one thing still bothers me: why doesn't he care about the fate of Rajiv Gandhi?

. . .

Come to live out a temptation! Every time I return from Cuba, I find myself sounding like a tourist brochure. Cuba is one of the biggest surprises in the modern world, if only because it has occupied a black hole in our consciousness for so long. If people think of the island at all these days, they probably think of army fatigues, warlike rhetoric, and bearded threats to our peace. Few people recall that Cuba is, in fact, the largest island in the Greater Antilles and, as even my sour guidebooks admits, "the most varied and most beautiful." That it has 4,500 miles of beach, nearly all of them as empty as a private hideaway. That there are more than eleven hours of sunshine on an average day, and the air is 77 degrees, the water even warmer. That it vibrates with the buoyancy of a late-night, passionate, reckless people whose warmth has only been intensified by adversity. And that it is still, apart from anything, a distinctly Caribbean place of lyricism and light, with music pulsing along its streets and lemon-yellow, sky-blue, alabaster-white buildings shining against a rich blue sea. Havana days are the softest I know, the golden light of dusk spangling the cool buildings in the tree-lined streets; Havana nights are the most vibrant and electric, with dark-eyed, scarlet girls leaning against the fins of chrome-polished '57 Chryslers under the floodlit mango trees of Prohibition-era nightclubs. Whatever else you may say about Cuba, you cannot fail to see why Christopher Columbus, upon landing on the soft-breezed isle, called it "the most beautiful land ever seen."

In Communist Cuba, of course, you will find shortages of everything except ironies. The Bay of Pigs is a beach resort now, and San Juan Hill is most famous for its "patio cabaret." The Isle of Youth, long the most dreaded Alcatraz in the Caribbean, entices visitors with its International Scuba-Diving Center. There is a "Cretins' Corner" in the Museum of the

Revolution, featuring an effigy of Ronald Reagan ("Thank you, cretin," says the sign, "for helping us strengthen the Revolution"). And one beach near Matanzas (the name means Massacres) has, somewhat less than romantically, been christened Playa Yugoslavia. Cuba, in fact, has edges and shadows not often found in other West Indian resorts: the billboards along the beach offer stern admonitions ("The best tan is acquired in movement"), and the gift stores in the hotels sell such deckchair classics as *The C.I.A. in Central America and the Caribbean.* Everything here takes on a somewhat unexpected air. "Cuba's waiting for you," runs the official tourist slogan. "We knew you were coming."

Cubatur's most intriguing attraction is undoubtedly its four-hour excursion each day to a psychiatric hospital. But when I asked one day if I could sign up for the tour, the laughing-eyed girl at the desk looked at me as if *I* were the madman. "It isn't happening," she said. "Does it ever happen?" "No," she replied, with a delighted smile.

Yet the seduction of Cuba, for me, lies precisely in that kind of impromptu roughness, and in the fact that its streets feel so deserted; the whole island has the ramshackle glamour of an abandoned stage set. Old Havana is a crooked maze of leafy parks and wrought-iron balconies, where men strum guitars in sun-splashed courtyards, inciting one to the pleasures of a life *alfresco*; its singular beauty, unmatched throughout the Caribbean, is that it feels as if it has been left behind by history, untouched. Here, one feels, is all the quaintness of New Orleans, with none of the self-admiration. And the freewheeling gaiety of a Sunday afternoon in Lenin Park, where soldiers twirl one another about to the happy rhythms of steel bands, is all the more intoxicating because it is so spontaneous; here, one feels, is all the hedonism of Rio with none of the self-consciousness. Everything in Cuba comes scribbled over with the neglected air of a Lonely Place; everything feels like a custom-made discovery.

The other great achievement of the Castro government, of course, is that its overnight arrest of history has left the island furnished with all the musty relics of the time when it was America's dream playground, and many parts of Cuba still look and feel like museum pieces of the American empire. Yes, there are troubadours' clubs, bohemian dives, a film school run by García Márquez, and a Humor Museum. But the most aromatic of the culture's features are, in many respects, the backward-looking ones: the savor of rum in the bars that Hemingway once haunted; the friendly dishevelment of the seaworn old Mafia hotels, crowded now with Oriental-featured tourists from Siberia; the rickety charm of white-shoe bands playing the theme from *The Godfather* in red-lit Polynesian restaurants that must have looked modern when first they were built, half a century ago. You can almost feel the city where typical honeymooners from Connecticut could stay at the Manhattan (or the New York) Hotel, take care of their needs at the Fifth Avenue Shoe Store, and cash their checks at one of the First National Bank of Boston's six local branches, before whiling away their evenings at the Infierno Club (or, in better circles, the Country Club). You can almost taste the tropicolored island where the Dodgers used to hold spring training and Fidel Castro was just another pitching prospect for the Washington Senators. You can almost hear Basil Woon exclaim, in his 1928 book, *When It's Cocktail Time in Cuba*, " 'Have one in Havana' seems to have become the winter slogan of the wealthy."

Yet it is something more than poignant memories, and something even deeper than sun-washed surfaces, that keeps me coming back to Cuba, and it is, I think, the fact that every moment is an adventure here, and every day is full of surprise. I never want to sleep in Cuba. And even after I have returned home—and the place has disappeared entirely from view—I find that it haunts me like a distant rumba: I can still hear the cigarette-voiced grandma in Artemisa who took me in from the rain and, over wine in tin cups, spun me family tales strange with magic realism, before leading me across puddles to hear Fidel; I can still taste the strawberry ice creams in Coppelia, where languorous Lolitas sashay through the night in off-the-shoulder T-shirts, beside them strutting Romeos as shiny as Italian loafers; I can still see the round-the-clock turmoil of carnival, and the Soviet doctor who sat next to me one year, blowing kisses at the dancers. Sometimes, when I go out at night and sit on the seawall alone, feeling the spray of the salt, the faint strumming of acoustic guitars carried on the wind, and the broad empty boulevards sweeping along the lovely curve of Havana Bay, I feel that I could never know a greater happiness.

Cuba, in fact, is in many of its moods the most infectiously exultant place I know: it sometimes feels as if the featureless gray blocks of Marxism have simply been set down, incongruously, on a sunny, swelling, multicolored quilt, so that much of the sauce and sensuality of the louche Havana of old keeps peeping through. "Every step I took offered up a new world of joys," wrote Thomas Merton, the Trappist monk, who felt himself a prince surrounded by graces "in that bright Island [where] kindness and solicitude surrounded me." Norman Lewis, after sixty-five years of traveling, told me that he had never found a place to compare with Havana. And even during these days of post-*glasnost* privations, the fact remains that windows are thrown open so that reggae floods the streets, and passengers waiting for a plane draw out guitars and improvise sing-alongs in the departure lounge. Many Cubans have made an art form of their appetite for wine, women, and song—all the more precious in the absence of everything else; one young friend of mine in Havana knows only four words of English, which he

59

repeats like a tonic each day, accompanied each time by a dazzling smile: "Don't worry! Be happy!" Very often, in fact, the island reminds me of that famous statement of the eighteenth-century Englishman Oliver Edwards: "I have tried, too, in my time to be a philosopher; but I don't know how, cheerfulness was always breaking in."

This exhilarating sense of openness hit me the minute I landed in Havana on a recent trip: the customs officials in the airport were dressed in khaki but winkingly turned the other eye whenever they saw cases piled high with fifteen pairs of new ready-for-the-black-market jeans; the immigrations officials, when not cross-questioning tourists, made kissing noises at their female colleagues. Out in the streets, I was instantly back inside some romantic thriller, with crimes and liaisons in the air. Dolled-up señoritas looked at me with the sly intimacy of long-lost friends; rum-husky men invited me into their lives.

By the following night, I was sitting along the seawall with a group of earnest students eager to thrash out Hermann Hesse, Tracy Chapman, yoga, Henry Fielding, and liberation theology. Later, walking past the commercial buildings of La Rampa, I heard the joyous rasp of a saxophone and, following my ears through the video banks and rainbowed portraits of the Cuba Pavilion, found myself in a huge open-air disco, free (like most museums, concerts, and ball games in Cuba) and alive with teenagers jiving along to a Springsteenish band in WE STICK TO FIDEL headbands and Che Guevara T-shirts; thus—the government hopes—are party-loving kids turned into Party-loving comrades. When the concert ended, round about midnight, I walked over to the ten-stool bar in the old Hotel Nacional, where four cheery, red-faced Soviets were singing melancholy Russian ballads to a flirty *mulatta* of quick charm. The girl counted off a few numbers on her long pink nails, then swiveled into action. "Ivan, Ivan," she cooed across at a lugubrious-looking reveler, "why don't you dance with me? Ivan, don't you like me?" At which Ivan lumbered up, popped a coin into the prehistoric Wurlitzer, and, as "Guantanamera" came up, threw his hands in the air and began wriggling in place with all the unlikely grace of a bear in a John Travolta suit. This, I realized, was not Club Med.

The country's beaches—289 of them in all—start just twenty minutes from the capital. At Santa María del Mar, a virtual suburb of Havana, lies one of the loveliest, and emptiest, strips of sand you'll ever see, with only a few old men—salty castaways from Hemingway—standing bare-chested in the water, trousers rolled up to their knees, unreeling silver fish. Behind them, across a road, reclines a typical Cuban seaside hotel, filled as always with something of the plaintiveness of an Olympics facility two decades after the games have ended. Inside its once-futuristic ramps, bulletin boards crowded with eager notices as happily crayoned as a child's birthday card invite foreigners to "Workers Shows" ("a very nice activity," offers the unread board, "where you will see the workers become artists for your pleasure") and "Happy Shows." Every Monday, at 4:30, there are "Cocktail Lessons," and every afternoon, "Music, Dance and Many Surprises." But when I looked at my watch, I realized it was 4:45, and Monday, and not a single cocktail student, not a sign of music or dance was in sight; somehow, in Cuba, it is always out-of-season.

The proudest attraction of the Cubatur office—and its brightest hope for gaining needed dollars—is the string of coral keys that sparkle like teardrops off the coast. One day I took the flight to Cayo Largo, an absurdly beautiful stretch of fifteen miles of open beach, graced with every enticement this side of Lauren Bacall. As soon as I got off the plane, at 8:45 a.m., I was greeted with a frenzied Cuban dance band and—what else?—

a Welcome Cocktail; for the rest of the day, I simply lay on the
beach and gazed at the cloudless line of primary colors—aqua
and emerald and milky green, flawless as a Bacardi ad. There
is nothing much to see in Cayo Largo, save for some basins full
of turtles and an island featuring 250 iguanas; but, as with all
the most delectable resorts in Cuba, the place is utterly empty,
even of Bulgarians in string vests. (This is, in part, because
locals are not permitted on the beach—this is, alas, no legal
fiction: I, too, while walking along the beach one drowsy Sunday
morning, was hauled over, by a policeman hiding in the bushes,
on suspicion of being a Cuban.)

In recent years, in a bid to rescue its shattered economy,
Cuba has begun refurbishing its old hotels with tiled patios and
stained-glass windows, and trying to entice visitors with "Afro
Shows" and "Smashed Potatoes"; but even now, thank Marx,
the island remains roughly 90 percent tourist-proof: one still
needs two chits and a passport to buy a Coca-Cola, and as in
some loony lottery, Visa cards are accepted only if they contain
certain numbers. This, though, is part of the delight of the
place: whenever one goes out at night, one never knows how
the evening will end, or when. Days are seldom clearer. One
sleepy Sunday not so long ago, I waited for a taxi to take me
back to Havana from the beach; and waited, and waited, and
waited, for three and a quarter hours in all, under a tree, on a
hot afternoon. Finally, just as I was about to lose all hope, up
lurched a coughing red-and-white 1952 Plymouth, with "The
Vampire Road" written across its back window. Seven exhausted souls piled into the wreck, and the next thing I knew,
the quartet in back was pounding out an ad hoc beat on the seat
and breaking into an a cappella melody of their own invention—
"Ba ba ba, we're going to Havana . . . ba ba ba, in a really sick
old car . . ." For the next two hours, the increasingly out-of-
tune singers unsteadily passed a huge bottle of rum back and

forth and shouted out songs of an indeterminate obscenity, while the mustachioed driver poked me in the ribs and cackled with delight.

In Santiago de Cuba, the second city of the island and the only officially designated "Hero City" of the Revolution, I spent a few days in the gutted home of a former captain of Fidel's. From the hills above, where Castro and his guerrillas once gathered, the city looked as it might on some ancient, yellowing Spanish map; down below, in a peeling room that I shared with a snuffling wild pig who was due to be my dinner, things were somewhat less exalted. Every night, in the half-lit gloom of his bare, high-ceilinged room, decorated only with a few black-and-white snapshots of his youth, my host took me aside ("Let me tell you, Pico Eagle . . .") and told me stories of the Revolution, then delivered heartbroken obituaries for his country. Next door, in an even darker room, one of his sons prepared dolls for a *santería* ceremony, the local equivalent of voodoo. And when it came time for me to leave, the old man asked for some baseball magazines from the States. Any special kind? I asked. "No," he said softly. "But I like the ones with Jackie Robinson in them."

That sense of wistfulness, of a life arrested in midbreath, is everywhere in Cuba: in the brochures of the once-elegant Hotel Riviera, which now, disconcertingly, offers a "diaphanous dining-room"; in the boarded-up stores whose names conjure up a vanished era of cosmopolitanism—the Sublime, the Fin-de-Siècle, Roseland, Indochina; in the Esperanto Association that stands across from a dingy, closed-off building under the forlorn legend R.C.A. VICTOR. Hemingway's house in the hills is kept exactly the way he left it at his departure almost thirty years ago—unread copies of *Field & Stream* and *Sports Illustrated* scattered across his bed—and the buildings all around, unpainted, unrepaired, speak also of departed hopes. One reason so many Cubans ask a foreigner, *"Que hora es?"* is to strike up a conversation—and a deal; another, though, is that they really do need to know the time in a place where all the clocks are stopped. Perhaps the most haunting site in the beach resort of Varadero is Las Americas, the lonely mansion above the sea built by the Du Ponts. Nowadays it is a dilapidated boarding school of a place, all long corridors and locked doors. The Carrara marble floor is thick with dust, and the photos in the drawing room are hard to make out in the feeble light. But along the mahogany and cedar walls there still hangs a tapestry poignantly transcribing all the lines of the poem that once contained the hopes the home embodied: "In Xanadu did Kubla Khan a stately pleasure dome decree . . ."

It is that mix of elegy and carnival that defines Cuba for me, and it is that sense of sunlit sadness that makes it, in the end, the most emotionally involving—and unsettling—place I know; Cuba catches my heart, then makes me count the cost of that enchantment. Cuba is old ladies in rocking chairs on their verandas in the twilight, dabbing their eyes as their grandchildren explain their latest dreams of escape, and the azure sea flashing in the background; it is pretty, laughing kids dancing all night in the boisterous cabarets and then confiding, matter-of-factly, "Our lives here are like in Dante's *Inferno*." It is smiles, and open doors, and policemen lurking in the corners; lazy days on ill-paved streets and a friend who asks if he might possibly steal my passport.

In Cuba, the tourist's thrilling adventures have stakes he cannot fathom. And every encounter leaves one only deeper in the shadows. My first night in a big hotel, a girl I had never met rang me up and asked, sight unseen, if I would marry her. The next day, in the cathedral, a small old man with shining eyes came up to me and began talking of his family, his faith, his grade-school daughter. "I call her Elizabeth," he said. "Like

a queen." He paused. "A poor queen"—he smiled ruefully—
"but to me she is still a queen." When we met again, at an
Easter Sunday mass, he gave me Mother's Day gifts for my
mother and, moist-eyed, a letter for his own mother in the
States. Only much later, when I got home, did I find that the
letter was in fact addressed to the State Department, and the
kindly old man a would-be defector.

And one sunny afternoon in a dark Havana bar, so dark that
I could not see my companion's face except when she lit a match
for a cigarette, I asked a friend if I could send her anything from
the States. Not really, she said, this intelligent twenty-three-
year-old who knew me well: just a Donald Duck sticker for her
fridge. Nothing else? I asked. Well, maybe a Mickey Mouse
postcard: that was quite a status symbol over here. And that
was all? Yes, she said—oh, and one more thing: a job, please,
with the CIA.

# ROCK 'N' ROLL GHOST TOWN

Even now, I find myself going back and back to Iceland in my mind, walking through its chilly, ghostly streets, pale even after midnight in the summer, and hushed, no dark to be seen for 2,400 hours or more. Somehow it is always half-light in the Iceland of my memories, and I am walking across empty fields, alone, the sun landing on the sea at 1:00 a.m. and then, after settling there for an hour or so, rising again as I walk back through the pallid light and hitch a ride on an early milk truck, round and around the cloud-covered coast. It seems as if I am always lost in the ice-blue poems of the Icelandic Romantics, and the images from the light nights that I spent there keep returning: the man with the chalk-white face who accosted me in the café of a lonely fishing village sometime after midnight and told me, through piercing eyes, of his dreams of Jesus and a flock of angels robed in white; the girl with the intense Egyptian gaze who picked me up my first day in the capital and transported me off into her visions of Tibet; the pilot of the six-seat plane who consulted his map as we flew, just the two of us, low over icefields and snow-capped peaks, to the deserted fjords of the west. Somehow I am always visiting Iceland in my memories, standing on a hill in the golden quiet, my shadow stretching for forty feet or more, then walking through a sleeping world in the dove-gray light of 2:00 a.m.

Perhaps it is because it is so otherworldly that Iceland leaves such an impression on the mind, because it feels so little like the planet that we know; days spent there are interludes from life, sojourns in some other, nether twilight of the mind. I knew, before I visited, a little about the epidemic oddness of the place: there was no beer in Iceland in 1987, and no television on Thursdays; there were almost no trees, and no vegetables. Iceland is an ungodly wasteland of volcanoes and tundra and Geysir, the mother of all geysers, a country so lunar that NASA astronauts did their training there; a place of fumaroles and solfataras, with more hot springs and mud pools and steam holes than any other wilderness on earth. One day I saw a crowd gathered on a Reykjavik street and looked in to see what they were staring at: it was a dog (long illegal in the capital). Iceland is a duck-shaped island with eight million puffins and a thirteen-hand horse that can not only canter and gallop but *tölt*.

Even "civilization" seems to offer no purchase for the mind here: nothing quite makes sense. Iceland boasts the largest number of poets, presses, and readers per capita in the world: Reykjavik, a town smaller than Rancho Cucamonga, California, has five daily newspapers, and to match the literary production of Iceland, the U.S. would have to publish twelve hundred new books *a day*. Iceland has the oldest living language in Europe— its people read the medieval sagas as if they were tomorrow's newspaper—and all new concepts, such as "radio" and "telephone," are given poetical medieval equivalents. Roughly three eldest children in every four are illegitimate here, and because every son of Kristjan is called Kristjansson, and every daughter Kristjansdóttir, mothers always have different surnames from their children (and in any case are rarely living with the fathers).

Every citizen of Iceland—even an erstwhile Wu Ziyang—must acquire a traditional Icelandic name, and the only exception ever made to this—for Vladimir Ashkenazy—prompted one disgruntled Spanish exile to ask if he could take on the new Icelandic name Vladimir Ashkenazy. People are listed in the phone book by their first names, which does not make life easy when the Jons alone take up thirty columns of the directory (the Hotel section of the yellow pages does not even fill a column).

Iceland is one of the largest islands in the world and, at the same time, one of the smallest worlds in the island, so intimate that it has the same kind of tranquil dottiness as the northern village in the movie *Local Hero*, in which every day promises to fetch up enigmatic mermaids, unlikely rock 'n' roll bands, and the same faces that you saw yesterday, and the day before. The first day I ever spent in "Surprise City" (as Reykjavik is called), I found golden-haired princesses and sword-wielding knights enacting fairy-tale sagas on the main bridge in the capital; I came within two feet of the president (who seemed, unguarded in the street, just another elegant blond single mother); and while staring at some man-sized chess pieces in the center of town, I was interviewed by the biggest daily newspaper, *Morgunbladid*, so astonished were its reporters to see a foreign face. The Salvation Army hostel is only four doors away from the Parliament building here, and the Parliament building itself is a modest two-story house with a doorman less imposing than those in the nearby pubs. Prisoners are allowed to go home for the holidays, and on the main road out of town you can still see the country's Nobel laureate in literature, Halldór Laxness, active at the age of eighty-nine.

Yet there is something deeper about the uncanniness of the place; something arising from its silences and space. You can feel it in the contained intensity of many people here, in the enormous calm with which they say *Já* and in the echoing way they say nothing at all. You can see it in their eyes, as shockingly beautiful, often, and as blue, as the sea when suddenly glimpsed around mountain curves. You can sense it in the almost archetypical elementalism of the place, where honey-cheeked beauty queens rub cheeks with hatchet-faced yahoos (it is, as Jan Morris saw, the perfect setting for Beauty and the Beast); you can feel it in the settledness of the place, the weighty sense of *gravitas*. It is easy to believe, in this uninhabited space, that you are living once more amidst the mead halls and monsters of *Beowulf*, within a tiny circle of light surrounded by an encroaching dark; it is easy to believe that the Irish hermits and Viking warriors who were the earliest settlers on the island still possess it with their ascetic calm and violence. There is something allegorical—not quite real—about the place that inspired Hobbitland and Wagner's *Ring*. Jules Verne's explorers came here to find the center of the earth; Iceland was, in the Middle Ages, the literal location of Hell. And for the Nazis, its pure-blond racial clarity made it a kind of Aryan paradise (*"Für uns,"* said one German, *"Island ist das Land"*). Iceland may be many things, but it is not your average country.

It is always difficult, even dangerous, to return to a world that has transported you, and epiphanies rarely repeat themselves. Yet I was determined to see Iceland outside the spell of its midsummer nights' dreams, in the lunar segment of its cycle. Not long ago, therefore, I returned to the place I had kept dreaming about. Icelandair is the only carrier that flies to Reykjavik from the U.S., linking its capital with Baltimore and, now, Orlando (as well as with New York). Keflavik Airport is the sole airport in Europe that has a duty-free shop for *arrivals*, and traditionally it was packed with Icelanders stocking up on beer. The most comfortable seats on Icelandair are in Saga Class, and its stunning cabin attendants sometimes wear black leather gloves. Many Americans know Iceland only as the place they were obliged to visit on what was, for years, the cheapest flight to Europe; now, ironically, Iceland is by some measures the most expensive country in the world (a fifteen-minute phone call to Japan cost me $175).

Yet nothing had prepared me for the biggest shock of all: when I stepped out of the airport, the whole place was dark. In all the time I had spent here, in the summer, I had never seen it dark. And darkness awakens something passionate and primeval in the land, some sense of buried intensity. Our bus bumped across the rainy emptiness, and here and there I saw a few modernist blocks and eerie, red-lit geodesic domes winking in the blue-black sky: a high-tech, lit-up vision of surreal desolation. Reykjavik, at eight-thirty in the morning, was cradled in a northern silence. There was an extraordinary stillness to the place, as if it were held in suspended animation, its red roofs shining placid in the unpolluted sky. The overwhelming impression, on the tiny, empty street where I was staying, was of silence and of dark.

It is, of course, the changes that one notices first whenever one comes back to any place, and it did not take me long to find that beer is legal now and that there are two television stations, broadcasting even on Thursdays. I saw an *I Was a Teenage Zombie* album amidst the slabs of strange fish and jars of bee pollen in the Reykjavik Flea Market (held every Saturday in an underground garage beneath the central bank); and Filipino women in flowing Islamic robes were walking down the street. The Holiday Inn has come to Reykjavik, and the Hard Rock Cafe; there is karaoke, too, and neon. Yet still, again and again, I felt I was in a kind of Alice Wonderland. Soon after arrival, I rang up to ask about a day trip to Greenland; the eight-hour tour cost $460. I called for a cab and was picked up by a hearty, shining matron driving a Mercedes. I walked into the Hotel

Loftleidir for lunch and there was Anatoly Karpov, former chess champion of the world, sitting in a ring of light at one end of an auditorium, above a tiny chessboard, watched by eight old men in anoraks. Two hours later, I was being harassed by a Greenlandic dancer with black stripes down his face and a clothespin in his mouth, which he kept pushing in and out at me.

By any standards other than the Icelandic, Reykjavik is still a quaint and quiet place, as silent as a photograph. It resembles, like most of the settlements in Iceland, a kind of Lego town— rows of tiny, clean white boxes set out in geometric grids, with roofs of red and blue and green. Much of the country feels as if it were made for children—even the ponytailed boys and ring-nosed girls are pushing baby strollers—and Reykjavik might almost be a small child's toy, as clean and perfect as a ship inside a bottle. Iceland is famous for having no mansions and no slums ("There is no architecture here," complained W. H. Auden), in much the same way as its language has no accents and no dialects: with a population smaller than that of Colorado Springs, uniformity is not hard to achieve. And because nearly all the houses are geothermically heated, the city whose name means Smoky Bay shines silent in the smokeless air, as clear as if seen through panes of polished glass. Reykjavik is one place where it really is worth climbing the steeple of the highest church to see the city, mute and motionless, laid out against the silver sea.

Yet it is not because of the capital but in spite of it that most visitors come to Iceland, and it is desolation that they seek and find. More than 80 percent of the country consists of ice fields, tundra, lava fields, and barren mountains, and huge stretches are as blank and inhospitable as anything in the Australian Outback. Such settlements as do exist look like suburbs in search of a city—a solitary farmstead here, a lonely lighthouse there, occasionally an isolated steeple: a small huddle of concrete inside a giant's rough paw. Nature adores a vacuum here. And the ground itself is like nothing so much as a geologist's textbook, a pockmarked mess of volcanic craters and hissing plumes of smoke till it looks as if the earth itself is blowing off steam, and the soil in parts is so hot that, only a few inches down, you can actually boil an egg. In Iceland, in John McPhee's happy phrase, "the earth is full of adjustments, like a settling stomach."

The largest glacier in Europe (more than three times the size of Luxembourg) is somewhere in this nothingness, and the largest lava field in the world; the oldest parliament in Europe was set up on this youngest soil. Samuel Johnson used to boast of reciting a whole chapter of *The Natural History of Iceland* from the Danish of Horrebow. That was Chapter LXXII, "Concerning snakes." It reads, in its entirety: "There are no snakes to be met with throughout the whole island."

The other factor that accentuates the bleak and weather-beaten beauty is the climate: in October there is already a wild white quilt swaddling the countryside, and the sun shines silver over silver lakes, the view from a bus identical to that from a plane thirty thousand feet above the Pole. Icelanders will tell you that, because of the North Atlantic Drift, the country has no extremes of temperature: many years see no snow at all in Reykjavik, and the lowest temperature recorded in the capital in thirty years is − 15° Fahrenheit. But no extremes of temperature, in my book, means that it is never, ever warm. In summer, when I visited, people were complaining of a heat wave when the temperature hit a chilly 54°; by early fall, bitter winds were whipping through the silent streets, slapping my face and almost knocking me off my feet. A local friend told me that he had been to Stockholm once and almost suffocated in the sweltering 64° heat. He couldn't wait, he said, to "get back to my cold Iceland."

In such an unaccommodating world, it is not surprising that visitors are often as unorthodox, in their way, as locals. ("Whenever I meet a foreigner here," an Icelandic girl told me in a disco, "I ask him, 'Why do you come to Iceland?' It is cold; it is expensive; and the people, they are closed.") Yet the country seems to bring out something pure in visitors, something a little bit out of the ordinary. The most luminous translations of modern Icelandic poetry into English, for example, were composed by a recent U.S. ambassador to Iceland, Marshall Brement, who has written beautifully of how Icelanders were the great European poets of the twelfth and thirteenth centuries and how even now, on one night a year, every member of Parliament must speak in rhyme. And though the island's attraction to photographers (Eliot Porter) and to poets (from Auden and MacNeice to Leithauser) may be self-evident, it seems to evoke something poetic even in an everyman. I once asked a young Danish student, who had chosen to live here for a year, what was the most exciting thing to do in Reykjavik. He thought for a long, long time. Then, a little sheepish, he replied, "Well, for me, I like walking at night in the Old Town, seeing the old houses. Or if you can go a little bit out of Reykjavik, if it is cold, like tonight, you can see the northern lights." The most beautiful place he had ever seen, he said, was Greenland. "It is so rich, in many ways. When you walk there, you see more clearly, you think more easily. Here it is a little bit the same."

That kind of calm transparency is, inevitably, harder and harder to maintain as the villages of Iceland get drawn into the shrinking global village. For ten centuries now, the island has preserved its own culture and its Old Norse diphthongs by living apart from the world, remote from changing realities. For centuries, Iceland has been a kind of hermit among nations, a private, inward-looking Lonely Place of fishermen and visionaries and poets. The pursuits for which it has been famous are largely solitary ones, made to ward off months of winter dark: thus the land with a population smaller than that of Corpus Christi, Texas, boasts six chess grandmasters and recently placed first in the World Contract Bridge Championship. The most famous Icelander in England, Magnus Magnusson, is, appropriately enough, the host of a fiendishly difficult quiz show, *Mastermind* (there are now fifty-three Magnus Magnussons in the country's phone book). Iceland is a kind of conscientious objector to modernity, out of it in all the right ways and priding itself on being a sort of no-man's-land in the middle of nowhere (and nowhen), a quiet neutral zone far from superpower rivalries: midway between Moscow and Manhattan, halfway between medievalism and modernity, it had its two moments of ambiguous fame—in 1972, when it was the site of the Boris Spassky–Bobby Fischer chess championship, and in 1986, when it was the safe house where Reagan and Gorbachev met and almost abandoned nuclear weapons. The miracle of Iceland is not just that, as Auden wrote, "any average educated person one meets can turn out competent verse" (and a kitchen maid he met gave "an excellent criticism of a medieval saga") but that the verse itself is devilishly complex, bristling with alliteration and internal rhyme, trickier than a sonnet. That tangled, palindromic, old-fashioned kind of rime has become almost a model for the country.

Now, though, increasingly, that legacy is threatened. Scarcely a century ago, only 5 percent of Icelanders lived in towns; today, the figure is more than 80 percent. For nine centuries almost, the population scarcely rose (it hit six figures only in this century); and as recently as 1806, there were only 300 citizens in Reykjavik, of whom 27 were in jail for public drunkenness. Today, however, 145,000 of the country's 255,000 people live in or around the suburb-sprouting capital. And the single foot of television alone has inevitably cast a shadow over a world in which lighthouse keepers read Shakespeare to fishing fleets and families wax Homeric in the dark. Though the government has worked overtime to protect its culture (hence the longtime ban on daytime television, and no broadcasting in the month of July), its efforts have often been in vain: Iceland (which seems to lead the world in leading the world in categories) now boasts more VCRs per household than any other country. In the Westman Isles, the rock formation that used to be called Cleopatra is now known by some as Marge Simpson, and the fishing crates nearby are decorated with portraits of the Teenage Mutant Ninja Turtles. Even young couples, when not talking of their holidays in Spain and their dreams of seeing the Pyramids, will tell you that purity is to be found now only in the countryside; that Reykjavik is dangerous and full of drugs; that, sadly, people use the word "cassette" instead of its Icelandic equivalent.

Iceland is also more and more full of foreign faces and less militantly blond than even four years ago. There is a Thai restaurant now in Reykjavik, and a Thai snack bar (complete with Buddha, picture of King Bhumibol, and sign for Coke in Thai); there are Somalian refugees, adopted kids from Sri Lanka, even immigrants from North Africa (whose children must—by law— be given names like Bjorn and Gudrun). In one factory alone, there are ten "mail order brides," three of them cousins from the Philippines. None of this would seem exceptional except in a country where, until recently, many people could hardly imagine Somalia, or Sri Lanka, or even California. When I was here in 1987, I found myself an object of dark fascination to people who could hardly tell an Indian from a Indianan; now, when I went to restaurants, I was greeted with a polite, unsurprised *Godan dag* in Icelandic.

The zealously maintained racial purity of the people has, of course, a shadow side: Hitler's *Mein Kampf* appears in the window of a local bookstore, and D. ÜBER ALLES has been scribbled up on walls downtown. Many Icelanders draw their imaginations tightly round themselves. One day an emaciated young ship's cook with nicotine-stained teeth leaned over to me in a café. He had been to Japan, he said, and China, and Baltimore. Which was his favorite place? He thought for a long time. "Holland. Is okay. And Norway and Denmark. Okay, but expensive." Was he preparing now for his next trip? "No," he said matter-of-factly. "I am an alcoholic. And on the ship I cannot go to A.A. meetings." Some Icelanders in the countryside still live in fear of a Turkish attack (there was one as recently as 1627).

At the same time, of course, the isolation that is so transporting to the foreigner is desperately confining to the would-be with-it teenager, and if Iceland seems very far from the world, the world can seem very far from Iceland. In Iceland, again by law, most shops and offices must bear Icelandic names, and the hotels—aimed at foreigners—are duly given unpronounceable names like Esja, Gardur, Ódinsvé. Yet more and more of the names used for recreation—aimed at the locals— bespeak a longing for abroad. The famous discos in Reykjavik have been Berlin, Hollywood, Casablanca, and Broadway; the new places to eat are Asia, Shanghai, Tokyo, and Siam. One of the trendiest joints in town is the L.A. Café; people downtown gather round the Texas snack bar. None of this would have much significance except in a culture that sees its identity reflected in its names.

One day an old man who was loitering outside a video arcade came up to me near the entrance of Tomma Hamborgarar. "There is so much new here," he declared. "It is almost as if Iceland was built in 1900 and not ten centuries ago. I remember when I was a child, hearing about the fairies who lived in the fields and everywhere. And the ghosts." The ghosts, he added, "sometimes follow a family for two hundred years."

For visitors, however, there are still enough ghosts to fill another planet. A middle-aged matron invited me one night into her solemn, sepulchral parlor. The first things I saw when I entered were a book on the Gestapo and a picture of a sea-blue sprite hiding inside a waterfall. Her grandchildren came out to stare at me, and when I explained that I was from India, they confessed that they did not know if that was near Pluto or Neptune. Then I was asked what kind of music I would like to hear. Icelandic, I replied, and on came a blast of local heavy metal.

There is, in fact, a deafening strain of rock 'n' roll in Iceland, and it is the voice of kids banging their fists against the narrow limits of their culture. With so few people in so vast a space, both elements are intensified, extreme: "wild" applies as much to society as to nature here. Iceland, then, is an inspired setting for the Hard Rock Café. It is not just that the island used to have the two largest discos in Europe; or that its most famous recent export is the eccentric dance band the Sugarcubes ("I'd never been in a skyscraper place before," said their lead singer recently, after her first trip to Manhattan); or even that Amina, the belle of Carthage, was recently performing in Reykjavik. It is, rather, that rock 'n' roll is an almost primal statement of rebellion here, a spirit of release. It is the way the young advertise their impatience with the old ways and their hunger for the new. Garage bands are sizzling in Reykjavik, and local magazines are full of articles on such local heroes as Deep Jimi and the Zep Creams. The radio was blasting "Leader of the Pack" when I drove one night to Kringlan, the glittery new yupburb where the Hard Rock is situated, and inside which blondes in dark glasses and boys in ties were clapping along to "The Wall" and shouting out, in English, "Unbelievable!" and "Give me five!"

It is, in fact, easy to feel in Iceland that one is caught up in some homemade Arctic version of *American Graffiti.* The first time I visited the country, I could not believe the "cruising" rituals that filled even the tiniest places on every weekend night; in the small northern town of Akureyri I watched a whole procession of Pontiacs, Range Rovers, and Porsches circling the tiny central square till 4:00 a.m., teenagers hanging out of their windows; motorcycle gangs (called Sniglar, or Snails) revving up along the sidewalks; twelve-year-old boys crying out *Gledileg Jól* (Merry Christmas) in the golden evening light. But this was in the middle of the saturnalian summer, when everything is topsy-turvy, and golf tournaments start at midnight, and three-year-old toddlers caper around till one in the morning each night (or one at night each morning). This was the time of midsummer madness, when people believe that rolling naked in the dew will cure you of nineteen separate ailments and that you will be granted a wish if you walk naked in the grass or cross seven fences, collecting a flower at each one of them.

When I returned to Iceland in the dark, though, I found that the same furious rites were taking place even in the freezing cold, bodies jamming the narrow streets of Reykjavik, "Jumping Jack Flash" pouring out of their windows, the streets packed at 2:00 a.m., muscle cars burning rubber in the parking lots. Reykjavik on a Saturday night is a reeling madhouse of people puking, people barking, people lying flat out on the street, their beautiful faces shining with illicit glee. A local band was playing "Runaway" in the Gaukar á Stöng pub, and the girls at their tables were lip-synching every word, and when the group went into "Break on through to the other side . . ." the girls got up and started flinging their naked arms around, whirling themselves into a bacchic frenzy, long hair and short skirts flying, like nothing so much as the Dionysian revelers in Oliver Stone's *The Doors.*

Sex? asked Auden in *Letters from Iceland.* "Uninhibited." And that was fifty-five years ago! Iceland discos, it seems safe to say, are not for the faint of heart. "I started smoking when I was ten, gave up when I was eleven, started again when I was twelve," a hard-drinking girl of nineteen told me, while her friend started raving about her holiday in Bulgaria; around us, various boys were burping, dancing on the table, and pursuing rites of courtship in which solicitations came well before intro-ductions. "These men do not have any behavior," a young Dan-ish boy standing near me remarked. "They are not even having a funny time." Later, I found there was a subtext to his com-plaint. "I went with four girls to the Moulin Rouge," he re-ported, "and all the men were blinking at me." After the discos close, at 3:00 a.m., everyone who is not in somebody else's arms (and even some who are) staggers off to swim naked in one of the city's open-air pools. I'M ICELANDIC, says a local T-shirt. WHAT'S YOUR EXCUSE?

Yet still, for all these odd eruptions, there is a kind of inno-cence in Iceland—an innocence almost betrayed by that longing for sophistication—and it is one of those places that are difficult to dislike. Even now, it seems to belong as much to Hans Christian Andersen as to Tolkien, and Peer Gynt's angels are as much in evidence as Axl Rose's. The most elegant hotel in Reykjavik puts a single lighted candle on its reception desk at nightfall. The waitress at the Shanghai restaurant is a classic Nordic beauty, with long Godiva tresses falling over her Chi-nese page-boy suit. ("The good children do get ice-cream as dessert," promises the menu, "with regards from Shanghai.") Many telephone numbers here have only five digits, and a child's painting of a rainbow that I saw in the National Art

Gallery had only four (not very vibrant) colors. Sometimes you're walking down the main street in the capital, and out of nowhere you come across a statue of a bear, dukes up, above the legend BERLIN 2380 KM. Everything's out of context here, simply because there is no context.

Much of Iceland still has the phlegmatic, Spartan style of the laconic north. The best hotels in Reykjavik offer little more than a bed, perhaps a TV, and a Bible in Icelandic (with a separate New Testament in German, French, and English); in rural areas, visitors generally stay in boarding schools. The museum in Akranes, the finest I saw in the country, displays a dentist's drill. On Saturday nights, couples in cocktail dresses and suits munch on sheep's heads, ram's testicles, reindeer, and ptarmigan; Auden and MacNeice gnawed, less happily, on "half-dry, half-rotten shark." One Westman Islander told me that during the terrible volcano eruption of 1973, he went with his grandmother to the harbor, just in time to see the last fishing boat fleeing to the mainland. "Oh, well," the grandmother said as lava poured toward her, about to bury five hundred houses, "the last boat's gone. Let's go home and have a coffee."

Iceland has yet to lose this never-never quality; it is a cozy, friendly, Christmas-tree kind of place: even the chic black-leather girls who come into the cafés on Saturday afternoons are carrying bundles of babyhood in their arms. My old friend Kristín, now studying African dance, told me eagerly about her nine-year-old daughter's class in karate, and how both of them kept strong with regular doses of "fish oil" (Icelanders, by some counts, are the longest-living people in the world). "Families are so important here," I said. She looked surprised. "They are not everywhere?"

And somehow, in the windswept silences, so bare and broad that the mind takes flight, the close-knit purity of the people can work a curious kind of magic. Chill Lutheran bells awakoned me one ringing Sunday morning, and I went out into the quiet, rainy streets, empty save for a few children, and the smell of fresh-baked bread, and an old crone in earflaps, delivering the *Morgunbladid*. From inside the most modern church in town, I heard choirs singing hallelujahs in the cool, severely tall white nave. Hallgrimskirkja has the whitest, chastest interior I have ever seen, snow-capped islands misty through the windows behind its altar's cross. Across the street is the Einar Jónsson House, which opens up for two afternoons a week to disclose the late artist's mythopoeic sculptures and Blakean visions of angels and ascents to heaven, all white, but muscular and rugged.

And in the sepulchral silence and unearthly calm of Iceland, the religious impulse has room to stretch out and take wing and pick up light. The only thing I could find inside the reading pocket on an Icelandair domestic flight was a copy of the New Testament, and Van Morrison was singing "Whenever God Shines His Light" above the sober businessmen's breakfast at the Hotel Holt. The figure of Jesus in the Skálholt church is one of the most haunting apparitions I have ever seen, a dim blue figure, hardly corporeal, faint as a half-remembered dream, emerging from the wall to look out upon an ice-blue stained-glass window. One of my favorite Reykjavik restaurants is a medieval cavern underground, lit entirely by candles, its waiters wearing friars' robes as they serve you pan-fried puffin in the dark. If countries were writers, Iceland would, I think, be Peter Matthiessen (whose very name and face suggest the elemental north): craggy, weathered, close to earth and sea, yet lit up from within by a high fierce restlessness. And as we sailed through large caverns near the Westman Islands, the captain of my ship stopped our vessel and got out a flute and started playing Bach toccatas and "Amazing Grace." The high, angelic sounds echoed round and around the empty space.

81

Sometimes, I knew, the strangeness I found in Iceland existed only in my head. The flaxen-haired girls I took to be paragons of Icelandic purity turned out to be from Iowa, or Essex. I did, finally, spot a dog one day, though whether he had—by law—an Icelandic name, I do not know. Every day, in the lobby of my hotel, I saw an old man marching up and down in red ceremonial costume, carrying a huge bell. When I asked an Icelandic friend what arcane custom he embodied, she, not surprisingly, shrugged—unaware that he was, in fact, the Town Crier of Lambeth, in London, sent here by the British Department of Trade and Industry.

Other times, though, I knew that there was something going on in the chilly, haunted silences. After a while the preternatural stillness of the treeless wastes can get to you, and inside you, and you can feel a Brontëan wildness in the soil. With its uncommonly beautiful people, its island curiosity, its closeness to traditions and tales, Iceland resembles nowhere so much as Java, its spellbound air charged with an immanence of spirits. Cold winds whistle through rows of white crosses in the black moor outside Akranes. The distinctive feature of the Icelander, for Sir Richard Burton, was "the eye, dark and cold as a pebble—a mesmerist would despair at the first sight." From my bed, at night, I could see nothing but a white cross shining in the dark.

Something in Iceland arouses the most passionate feelings in me, and picks me up, and will not let me go. On my first trip to the island, disoriented by the never-ending light, I stayed awake all night in my hotel, uncharacteristically writing poems. But this time, too, in the emptiness and dark, I could not sleep, and found myself alone at night with feelings I could not scan, the wind so fierce outside my window it sounded like the sea. Sometimes it feels as if the forty miles or so that people can see across the glassy air here they can also see inside themselves, as if, in this penetrating emptiness, you are thrown down and down some inner well. Sometimes it feels as if the land itself invites you almost to see in its changing moods a reflection of your own and, in the turning of the seasons, some deeper, inner shift from light to dark.

"Especially at this time of year, people have many different feelings here," a car mechanic called Oluvi explained to me one night. "In the dark they have much time to think of God—and of other things in that direction."

The baying of dogs woke me up my first morning in Bhutan. Otherwise, the main town square outside my room was empty, and silent. A huge full moon sat atop the golden mountains in a sky already blue. To the west, strips of mist snaked in and out of the hills as if to heighten an air of unreality. Below, workers in hoods, carrying scythes—like refugees from some biblical tale—were marching towards the fields, and schoolchildren too, in their traditional gray-and-purple jerkins. Around the golden stupa at the edge of town there was already a loud muttering of monks, and old women in turquoise beads and plaits circling around, counting their rosaries as they walked, and candles fluttering in musty antechambers. Already, the warm Himalayan sun was bathing the medieval buildings in light.

Thimphu is the only real town in Bhutan, yet its population is no bigger than a crowd at Shea Stadium when the place is half empty. It takes just a morning to explore the capital. There is only one main street, and all its shops are numbered. One reason for the numbers, perhaps, is that all the names are identical. As soon as I walked out of the Druk Hotel, I came across the Druk Liquor Shop. Also the Druk Variety Corner. Just around the corner, Druk Jewelleries. A little farther down, the Druk Medical House (which specializes in shoes).

Just past the huge display of 1988 Thai Air advertisements that guards the Druk Hotel was the office of Druk Air, the national airline of Druk Yul (or the Land of the Thunder Dragon). Inside, however, there was little decoration. Just a Thai Air ashtray, a whole display of Thai Air destinations, and a life-size cardboard cutout of a Thai Air stewardess joining her hands together in the traditional Thai *wai* of greeting. I went into Yu-Druk Travel, but it was empty—save for a huge cardboard cutout of another Thai Air girl. I passed through a dark archway, over a plank placed above some sludge, up a narrow, unlit staircase, and past an enormous padlock, into the office of Tee Dee U Car Rental. Its main feature was a pretty picture of a Thai Air hostess bowing her respects. By eleven-fifteen on this weekday morning, a sign was already up outside Druk Consult: CLOSED FOR LUNCH 1–2:30.

Thimphu, I would later find, is a roaring, crowded, feverish metropolis by Bhutanese standards. By any other standards, it is a miracle of calm. Shopkeepers sat outside their stores, serenely knitting in the sun. Monks rested their heads on green benches in the plaza, soaking up the rays under a tall Swiss clock. At the town's main intersection—its only intersection, in fact—a policeman directed traffic with the straight-arm precision of an archer, hands extended toward the occasional car as if he were holding a bow. The only talkative things in Thimphu were the trash cans. WHOEVER YOU MAY BE, announced one receptacle of dirt, USE ME TO KEEP THE AREA CLEAN.

Under the startling blue of heady winter skies, I took in the exotic roll call of store names in what may well be the world's most indigenous land: Dolly Tshongkhang Shop No. 15, Sonam Rinchen Beer Agency cum Bar, Llendrup Tshongkhang Cement Agent (Shop No. 31, Thimphu), Tipsy Tipsy (Deals in Tipsy Extra Special; Tipsy Strong Beer). Many of them had a curious kind of offbeat innocence: Tshewang Fancy Store,

Spark Fashion Corner, Etho Metho Handicrafts, Hotel Sam Druk ("Fooding and Lodging"). Salesman: must look honest, pleaded a less than reassuring sign in one shop.

And though the most famous fact about the Forbidden Kingdom was its young king's love of professional basketball—the "Fearless Lion" could traditionally be seen almost every afternoon practicing jump shots in the middle of town, while dressed in ceremonial robes—there was not much hoop action in sight. The liveliest thing in town, in fact, seemed to be the posters of Phoebe Cates—Phoebe Cates pouting, Phoebe Cates smoldering, Phoebe Cates smiling. A local video store was advertising *Paradise*, starring Phoebe Cates. (If only, I thought, Phoebe Cates worked for Thai Air, how simple Bhutanese decoration would be!) And then, a little farther on, up a small rise, I saw an octagonal white cottage with a spotted red toadstool outside and cacti around its walls. Inside was a chuckling mechanical monkey that announced the time, a set of dollhouse chairs, a sign that said modus: cash-down, and a pink button with which one could summon the proprietor, a white-haired Swiss man who looked as if he were on his way to see the Brothers Grimm. Here at last was the most famous establishment in the "Land of Hidden Treasures": its only Swiss bakery!

Bhutan has long been celebrated as perhaps the ultimate Lonely Place in the world, a snow-capped Buddhist kingdom tucked away in the depths of the High Himalayas. For years at a time, nothing is heard of the secret land of archers. At the time I visited, Bhutan had no TV, no daily newspapers, no air links with the outside world save Dhaka and Calcutta; its Olympic athletes had never seen boats before they left the country, or high-rise buildings, or even crowds. And such was the isolation of the land that it seemed to belong to fairy tale. "Ghosts, witches and crawling spirits are so familiar that often valleys and settlements are named after them," noted a standard political survey of the country; early British explorers came back with tales of bloodthirsty arrow duels in which the spectators would tear out the liver of the loser, eat it with butter and sugar, mix the fat and blood with turpentine in order to produce candles, and turn the bones into pipes on which they could play strange melodies. Even relatively prosaic books like *Two and Two Halves to Bhutan*, a relentlessly matter-of-fact account of a British doctor taking his family (and a teddy bear called Aloysius) through the unpaved wilds of Bhutan during the 1960s, contained sentences like the following: "The head lama of the dzong, the omze, is assisted by a Lopon Kudung in charge of discipline; the champen instructs gaylongs in dances, music, reading and writing."

What facts did occasionally emerge from the sequestered kingdom, moreover, served only to confirm its air of otherworldliness. Bhutan had not been part of the Universal Postal Union until 1969, yet since then it had invented steel stamps, three-dimensional stamps, talking stamps (in the shape of records), and stamps made of silk. A woman I had never met, in Denmark, wrote to inform me that a man named Rob Roy had recently put on a production of *A Midsummer Night's Dream* in the remote Bhutanese settlement of Tashigang. A U.N. official in North Korea filled my ear with tales of the intoxicating substances grown by foreign advisers based in Thimphu. And at the Olympic Games in Seoul, mysterious snippets about Bhutan kept catching my eye: first, the secretary of the Bhutanese Olympic Committee acknowledged that "Many athletes thought we were in Central America or Africa," and then—not coincidentally, perhaps—an item in *The Olympic Villager* told how a Bhutanese guest of the Bhutan-Korea Friendship Society had gone into a local hairdresser requesting a "light wave on the side" and come away with an Afro. One month later, on the

"Descending Day of Lord Buddha from Heaven," just two weeks before the king's thirty-third birthday, on the day of the "Meeting of Nine Evils," word trickled out that His Majesty Jigme Singye Wangchuk, the "Precious Ruler of the Dragon People" and long the most eligible bachelor in Asia, had made formal his marriage to four local sisters (in part, perhaps, because they had already borne him eight children).

The most singular fact of all, though, was that Bhutan had never opened its doors to the world. Cut off entirely from planet Earth until a generation ago, Bhutan had always been an area so remote that it hardly seemed to appear on any maps. Taken over—and united—by a fleeing Tibetan lama in 1616, it had never enjoyed any contact with reality until, in the early nineteenth century, the British government in India had begun annexing it. After the Bhutanese retaliated, rejecting ultimatum after ultimatum, they were finally given some tribute in return for the territory and, in 1907, with the blessing of the British, they found themselves with a hereditary monarchy, ruled by King Ugyen Wangchuk (great-grandfather of the present king).

But having seen change come so violently to Tibet (when the Chinese invaded in 1950), and so suddenly to Sikkim (with the incorporation of the tiny kingdom into India in 1975), and so surreptitiously to Nepal (with the gradual influx of global villagers), the Hidden Kingdom had decided, in recent times, to barricade its doors ever faster. In all its history, Bhutan had never seen more tourists in a year than Disneyland sees in a single hour; its first and only foreign minister once told me that too many visitors were "not very high-class people." Just before I arrived, moreover, it had raised the price of entry for tourists to $250 a day and, in addition, forbidden all tourists from visiting the only tourist attractions in Bhutan—its monasteries. I, however, was in a special position. Because Bhutan depends so much on India for its independence, Indian passport holders are allowed to come and go in Bhutan as they please, to stay as long as they wish, to make themselves at home inside the world's remotest kingdom. It sounded to me like an irresistible opportunity: to live for a while, as a native, inside the "world's last Shangri-la."

So it was that one winter day I went along to the Calcutta office of Druk Air, to ask about buses to Bhutan. Locating at last the dusty staircase in an apartment building where the office is situated (squashed between the Royal Customs Office of Bhutan and the Consulate General of Bhutan), I waited for an hour outside an emphatically locked door. Then, suddenly, a large man with a heavy mountain air above his Lakers T-shirt appeared before me. Hurry, hurry, he said, the plane was leaving in two hours—maybe less. But I wanted to go by bus! Yes, yes, he said, but this was a special plane—the first jet ever to land in his country! The British Aerospace 146 had enjoyed its maiden flight just three days earlier, and upon landing in Bhutan had received a formal blessing and *shugdel* ceremony from the entire monk body (I later saw pictures of the occasion—a group of bewildered-looking Englishmen in ties, surrounded by chanting monks, all seated cross-legged on a runway in the middle of nowhere). Today was going to feature its first commercial flight! A once-in-a-lifetime opportunity, a historic occasion! If I didn't move quickly, I would have to go the usual way—on an aging, sixteen-seat propeller plane.

And so it was that one hour later, I found myself standing in Dum Dum Airport, in front of the booth that Druk Air shares with JAT (the Yugoslav airline), now entirely empty. And standing. And standing. Then I noticed a tiny line of Bhutanese passengers checking in at the Thai Air counter, down the hall. It seemed a simple enough procedure: hand the attendant your case, watch him smash himself in the leg, wait for his curses to subside, then proceed to the departure lounge. A few hours later, I joined twelve disoriented passengers scattered amidst the eighty seats of a spotless new $30 million jet, the fiery red-and-gold dragon of Bhutan leaping across its tail. "I'm in civil aviation," a Canadian next to me explained. "We're trying to make it safer to land in Bhutan." I see. "Yes," offered a Bhutanese man nearby. "They're only charging fifty percent for this flight. That's because there's only a fifty percent chance of surviving." Oh, really? "You see, the minimum for a safe landing is around four thousand feet," the civil aviation expert continued. And how long was the runway at Paro? "Around forty-two hundred feet." Oh, excellent.

Ahead of us all, as the plane took off, were the highest mountains in the world, mysterious and snow-capped in the blue, blue sky. Below us, a few huge monasteries—massive, white-washed, multistory fortresses—were tucked into the folds of lonely valleys. No roads were inscribed across the hills, no settlements or people: just huge white blocks in a sealed-off world, and shafts of sun like giant searchlights.

Slowly, almost shyly, the plane began to descend over mountains with monasteries perched improbably on their tops. Then, very slowly, it veered in upon a tiny opening in the mountains and touched down. Around us all, in the empty valley, was nothing but silence. A few villagers gathered wordlessly beside the two-room airport: pink-cheeked peasant women, runny-nosed toddlers with woolen caps pulled down over their eyes, sturdy men in multicolored dressing gowns. A girl called Karma, or Universal Law—the sister, it mysteriously appeared, of the Lakers-loving official in Calcutta—quietly checked us into the "Lotus Garden of the Gods." And then we were outside, in a Druk Air minibus (its only decoration, a sticker for Thai Air), and alone in a soundless world.

An hour or so later, the bus started up, and we set out on the winding two-hour trip into town, hugging the edges of the narrow mountain road. Occasionally, we passed buildings—giant, terraced Tudor-seeming fortresses, their shingled roofs held down with stones, their white plaster walls dotted with rows of perfect bay windows—twenty or thirty openings in all—and their frames painted with flowers or the tails of snarling dragons. Then night began to fall, and lights came on in the forbidding buildings, shining like candles in the dark.

Finally, we came round a corner, and there, before us, at our feet, was a fairyland of lights. We descended into the valley and drove past rows of many-windowed towers, as if into the heart of some enormous Christmas cake. Then the van stopped, a door opened, and I was released into the chilling night. The streets were cold and empty, save for a few hooded figures shuffling past. On every side stood heavy mountain fastnesses. A few faint lights shone in small arched windows. I was alone in a city of candles.

The only particular sights for a visitor to see in Bhutan are its dzongs, the huge whitewashed seventeenth-century fortresses cum monasteries cum administrative centers—constructed without nails or plans by the country's first Tibetan rulers—which tower above every settlement in the country and are themselves overbrooded by watchtowers. My second morning in Thimphu, therefore, I set off to visit Simtokha Dzong, which guards the hillside five kilometers out of town. Five kilometers—a little more than three miles—is, however, a long distance in Bhutan: three hours by foot, I was told, and roughly half an hour by car. (Yuri Gagarin had circumnavigated the globe before Bhutan had installed its first road.)

After wandering around in circles for a while, I came at last upon an ancient Indian Mahindra jeep, held together with bits of soggy tissue. The driver patted the dust off his front seat and, with a flourish, presented me with the place of honor beside him (a rather mixed blessing, I felt, since the person in the front seat had to enjoy the gearshift thrust between his legs). A woman—a rather thick peasant woman—bundled into the front seat beside me, one snot-nosed issue perched on her lap, another suckling furiously at her breast. Seven or eight other unfortunates piled into the gloom behind us. The woman held her nostrils and violently expelled the contents of her nose. A man behind me—rather inauspiciously, I thought—began muttering a series of prayers. The others tuned up with a preparatory series of coughs, groans, and sneezes. And so we rattled off toward the breakneck curves.

Above the mirror in the jeep were some Technicolor stickers of four-armed Hindu gods; along the dashboard were two soulful portraits of German shepherds and a sticker that said "1987 Visit Thailand Year." We drove past trucks that said "Ruff and Tuff," trucks with illuminated Buddhas on their foreheads, trucks with slanting Nepali eyes painted eerily above their headlights. Whenever the trucks passed by, so too, very often, did songs, as the passengers seated on sacks in the back sweetened their tortuous journey with song.

At one point, our driver braked suddenly and began fumbling desperately through a clangorous collection of antique wrenches and pliers kept below his seat. Then he got up, ambled over to a hut, and brought back some water. Opening the hood, he pressed the accelerator down with his hand, threw some water into his mouth, some more onto the engine, and some more in the direction of the thick woman's children. At this, the large family—to my relief—disembarked. Then we started up again, jolting past neat official signs, flowering gold lettering on crimson boards: National Mushroom Development Programme, National Stove Project Training Site, Office of the Gyalpoizimpa. We drove past women breaking rocks by the side of the road, past shepherds beating along their flocks of yaks, past colored banners that proclaimed: THERE IS NO CURE FOR AIDS BUT IT IS PREVENTABLE (to a people who, in six cases out of seven, could not read a word of anything, let alone English). Mostly, we went around curves. Sometimes, when we did, I was thrown on top of the driver, rendering him almost incapable of steering; sometimes I was pushed into the woman—or, after she left, towards the door. This was unfortunate, because the jeep had no door. It was also unsettling because there is an average of fifteen curves per kilometer in Bhutan (and foreigners in Bhutan measure direction in this way. "I covered 4,500 curves going across country," an intrepid sixty-year-old Englishwoman later told me, only to be put in her place by an international adviser who said, "That's nothing! I covered 5,500 on the round trip from Thimphu to Phuntsholing"). I began to miss my human cushion, the snorting madonna and child.

At one point, the driver jerked to a halt, and one of the passengers emerged from the back, eager to conquer the precipitous curves. Muttering an impromptu prayer above the steering wheel, he turned the key, pressed the clutch, and then, eyes wild, mouth bloodied by betel nut, lurched towards the chasm. Gears jammed, the jeep swerved madly between mountain face and precipice, and I recalled that the *Bhutan Motor Vehicles Act Parts I and II* was one volume that had never—I had checked—been taken out of the Thimphu Public Library. With a terrible convulsion, the jeep screeched to a halt, and the acolyte driver, muttering some term of hatred for the jeep in particular and the automotive industry in general, returned to the darkness in back. A man handed out some *paan* to calm all our nerves, and then we were off again, wheezing past prayer wheels painted with skulls, hills still radiant with gold and copper and green, wisp-bearded old men who seemed to be

walking across the whole country. THANKS, said signs as we left
little settlements, and SEE YOU AGAIN warned the mudguards
on jeeps.

And so it was almost every time I moved in Bhutan, where
trips are decidedly more a matter of traveling than arriving. If
I was lucky, public transportation meant my own size-nine feet,
laboring up mountains while shiny acronymed Land Cruisers
whooshed past (though sometimes, even in the tourist center
of Paro, on the only main road in the country, in the middle of
a weekday afternoon, I walked for more than an hour without
seeing a single vehicle). If I was unlucky, it meant a jeep, and
the stench of gasoline, the suffocating dust, the endless stops
and starts, the shriek of horns round every curve, the ritual
emptying of noses on the floor. If I was doomed, it meant a
local bus—known to foreigners as the "Vomit Express" (though
"Express," of course, was something of an embellishment).

Simtokha Dzong, when I arrived, was in a state of expectant
calm. Like most Bhutanese dzongs, and like the medieval monasteries they so strongly resemble, it had a school attached, and
now, in December, exams were drawing near. Everywhere I
looked—perched in trees, scattered across the hillside, wandering up and down the bending road—students in tartan tunics
were huddled over books or memorizing some ancient scripture. It was a noble sight, the brown-and-red-cloaked boys on
the rich golden hills, in the shadow of a whitewashed citadel
and a sky of guiltless blue. The students seemed a serious lot,
and theirs, I learned, was a singularly tough regimen. Every
day they had nine periods—in thirteen different subjects—as
well as one and a half hours of prayer at dawn, one and a half
more at night. Like all male Bhutanese, they were not allowed
to cover their knees—even in winter—until the head of the
monk body had done so. True to their country's highly tradi-

tional ways, they were also being taught classical dance, ancient methods of carving wooden blocks, and, especially, Bhutan's native Dzongkha language. As soon as the exams were over, they would do two weeks of "social"—cleaning the monastery and helping out around town—and then they would take two- or three-day bus trips back to their distant homes for the only vacation of the year. "Bhutan people say, 'Keep your cows at home, send your children to school,' " explained one of the students. "If the cows go far away, they will forget you. But if the children go, they will understand."

There was only one thirty-minute period for sports every day, he went on, and these consisted not of "football, volleyball, these kinds of modern sports, but old pastimes—like how to throw a dart." Just as he was saying this, I noticed some boys careening up and down the hillside in pursuit of dogs. A few mischievous characters were sheltering puppies in their cloaks, others were carrying them along by their ears. The whole mad chase was attended by much hilarity and yelping. I suspected that this might be one of the traditional sports. "Oh, no," cried my new friend. "These people"—he pointed to a Royal Government of Bhutan truck drawn up outside the monastery gates— "these people are coming to collect the dogs. You see, these dogs do many dirties here." "How many live in the dzong?" "One hundred." "One hundred?!" "Just now, they will be taken to the Indian border and let out there." "The Indian border! That's seven hours away!" "Oh, yes, very far."

Thus Bhutan could claim another export, and the most over-populated country in the world would find itself with one hundred more mouths to feed.

As soon as the commotion had subsided, and the truck pulled away with its yapping captives, I decided to make my first attempt on the dzong. When I approached, the young boys huddled over their books near the entrance assured me solemnly that I would need a permit. But a permit was nothing more than a nod of acquiescence from a rheumy-eyed caretaker who was sitting nearby in dirty robes. Within seconds, I was following him and a young monk through the entrance, our bare feet cold on the sunless stone. The old monk opened a huge dungeon door, and we found ourselves inside an enormous prayer hall. The place was dark, very dark, and empty. A golden Buddha sat before us, scarcely visible in the gloom. We walked in farther, and the darkness began to envelop us. There was nothing to see, nothing to hear—only the dark voices of the monks outside.

Coming out once more into the prayer hall, the caretaker led us through the chamber to another unlit antechamber, shiny elephant tusks placed like giant cashews at the feet of Avalokitesvara, Buddha, and Tara. Old scriptures were stacked in bundles on the floor. On every wall, black gods in necklaces of skulls were copulating with milk-white, red-tongued demons. The old monk began to chant, and suddenly we were in a different place; the silences were charged.

Then we came out again, past a locked door guarded by a skull-wreathed deity, and up to a dragon-headed shrine. The young monk slapped down a one-ngultrum note. The sage handed him three dice. Closing his eyes tightly, the young monk pressed the dice to his forehead, then shook and shook them in his hand. Then he deposited them on the altar. Once more, and again once more. The old monk considered the throws, said something brief, and then we were back out in the sun.

In the days that followed, I traveled to all the famous dzongs in Bhutan: to Paro Dzong, entered by crossing a medieval bridge and slipping in through a side gate; to ruined Drukgyel Dzong, the very picture of some aged European castle, all its windows gutted, and cluttered now with crows, to Punakha Dzong, the winter home of the principal monk body, a gay festival of bird song, of trees flowering as red as the monks' robes laid out along the riverbank outside—an Oxbridge college surprised in midsummer, so it seemed, a mild and light-filled place of tidy gardens and neat bridges, its green-and-golden-and-yellow-fringed prayer wheel shining in the sun; and to Ta Dzong, the whitewashed, spiral-staircased watchtower that is home now to the National Museum, and so to a piece of moon rock donated by Richard Nixon, and to mounted heads of a blue sheep, a golden cat, a black panther, and a golden takin, all leading to its crowning glory: an entire floor given over to a chapel and the country's stamps (though it must be said that Bhutan's famous stampmakers may be running out of subjects worthy of their art—the once-lofty celebrations of the United Nations, the Apollo space missions, and the paintings of da Vinci and van Gogh have now been replaced by commemorations of Princess Diana's babies, the two hundredth anniversary of manned balloon flights, and Donald Duck).

The central dzong in Bhutan, however—and the last word in Bhutanese vigilance—is the massive fortification at Tongsa, set in the very heart of the country, bestraddling the path that was once the country's only road and looking out over valley after valley after receding valley, all the way to the distant snowcaps. Tongsa Dzong is less a building than a whole town unto itself, courtyard leading to quadrangle, quadrangle to passageway, passageway to courtyard, stretching on and on and on, incorporating every last detail of daily life. Burgundy robes were laid out on the sun-baked stone to dry. Monks polished incense holders on the whitened terraces. Gaylongs, or young novices, went back and forth, hoisting cumbersome buckets of water.

Having penetrated the inner courtyard of this formidable place, I sat down to collect my thoughts. As soon as I took out my notebook, however, I noticed a little monk edging closer to take a look. And then another. Then two more. Then a gaggle of others, and then still more, until I was all but buried in a circle of red, scarcely able to go on writing because of the twenty-four tiny monks crowded around me. Feeling obliged somehow to provide a little entertainment, I set about drawing a raccoon. "Mouse." "Pussycat." "Bear," the monks cried out, rather undiplomatically, I thought. Somewhat piqued, I changed the game and began writing out the letters of the alphabet. A chorus rose up around me: ". . . B, C, D, E . . ." At this point, controversy broke out as to the correct order of the letters to come: "V, Q, W, E, G . . ."

The linguistic issue was still unresolved when someone spotted my Instamatic, presumably the only camera in central Bhutan. Asking if he could borrow it, the little monk set to clicking away at all his friends. They clicked away at him. Everyone clicked away at me. "Address, address," cried someone, and a tiny gaylong began copying out in my pad: "Gangchuk Monk Body, Tongsa, Bhutan." "Address, address," came the cry again, followed by more requests for my address, my name, for more raccoons. Never had my drawings been so popular! Then there came a high-pitched cry from an upper window: "Mr. Pico, Mr. Pico." I looked up, to see five impish faces peering down at me from the archways above. Two full pans of water came crashing down beside us.

Then, as if in atonement, or at least in repayment for the raccoons, the little monks led me into a central prayer hall, plopped themselves down above their texts, and began bawling out their chants, beaming at me as they did so and waving.

As soon as this traditional sport concluded, an eleven-year-old urchin who had learned English from a man called Cyrus presented himself as my companion for the day. Up and down the hills he led me, pointing out the cry of a deer, showing me a picture of Padmasambhava, the Indian mystic who had brought Buddhism to Bhutan in the eighth century, explaining the town's greatest attraction. "Nineteen eighty-seven Japanese lights! Last year, water was only up in there. Just now Japanese bring light there." "So now light no problem?" "No. One month now, no light." The gist of this confusing exchange became clear only when I returned to the huge and empty hilltop guesthouse that was my home in Tongsa. By five-thirty, it was pitch black. For the next fourteen hours, I was alone in the unlit and un-heated old building, able at last to see why my *Survey of Bhutan* had matter-of-factly announced, "Black magic is a part of Bhutanese life."

The greatest of all Bhutanese monuments however—its Potala Palace or Mont-Saint-Michel—is Taktsang, the temple perched improbably on the side of a three-thousand-foot sheer cliff, wedged into the side of the mountain like some bird of prey's high aerie (and known as the "Tiger's Nest" because it is be-lieved that Padmasambhava flew to this impossible site on the back of a tiger). Taktsang is, without doubt, one of the most remarkable places in the world, extraordinary enough to make Machu Picchu seem workaday. And its sense of miracle is inten-sified by the steep and arduous climb that every pilgrim must make to get there. I made the trip alone, one cloudy winter morning, accompanied only, now and then, by a toothless old man, almost as slow as I was, and his two ponies. The tinkle of their bells led me through woods, over streams, across creaking wooden bridges, through packs of snuffling wild boars. The climb seemed endless. Then at last, after ninety minutes, we reached an open space, a hilltop crisscrossed with dove-white prayer flags. There, ahead of us, was Taktsang. But as I climbed, it disappeared again, and then came back, and vanished once more, round every turn, until at last, an hour later, the "Temple of Heaven" announced itself with a clear-singing prayer wheel and the steady hiss of a waterfall. Arriving, near breathless, at the top, I felt like a conquering hero—until I recalled that some devout Bhutanese make the whole ascent on their stomachs, one full-length prostration following another for three weeks or more.

At the entrance, a few young monks looked out at me with the incredulity I felt I deserved. Then they led me into a compact prayer hall, its window open to the valley below. Rainbowed streamers fluttered from the ceiling. The sunlight flooded onto scalding *thankas* of wild-eyed demons and tongue-joined copulants. Orange flowers sat below pictures of orange-robed Buddhas. The waterfall sang, the cliffs plunged down, a few dirty-chinned little monks scampered up the dented logs that served as stairs. And as I left, I heard them singing from an upstairs window.

And so, in time, I came to settle into the rhythms of this silent country, to come to know its patterns so well that the days began to pick up speed and blur. At dawn, in Thimphu, the mist swaddling the western mountains. In the mornings, the quiet tennis-ball sound of wood being chopped outside my window. At lunch, in the hotel, a team of Japanese "salarymen" lined up in dark suits around a large table and muttering gloomily, *"Muzukashii desu, ne?"* ("It's difficult, isn't it?"), as they bravely did battle with their curries. At four o'clock, the officials streaming out of the cottagelike buildings in Tashichhodzong, the central government complex, like schoolboys just released from class, healthy young men, most of them, sturdy and solemn, bearing thick black briefcases, white scarves worn like sashes over tartan kilts. As darkness fell, the bright young things of Thimphu—all six of them—assembling in the Benez café to gossip about boyfriends, in the "convent English" of wealthy girls from private Indian schools. And then, after dark, lights shining like candles in the many-windowed houses, and the streets all chill and silent. All night, the yelping of the mangy dogs, and then, at dawn, the light returning with the sound of jeeps, a reveille of horns, the clatter of boxes loaded onto trucks.

And gradually, as the days went on, I began to make a life inside this Sleepy Hollow world. I took over a small room in the Druk Hotel. I signed on as a member of the Thimphu Public Library. I bought balcony tickets to Stallone movies at the local cinema (where the crowd seemed especially taken with Terry Funk, in the part of Frankie the Thumper). And I took my clothes to the town's dry cleaner—less deterred than I should have been, perhaps, by its enigmatic motto, "Cleanliness before Loveliness"—and bargained the proprietress down to an express seven-day service.

Sometimes I moved to Paro and adjusted myself to its bucolic, mild-breezed rhythms. In the mornings, when I awoke, girls singing as they worked. Afternoons in Paro Dzong, all red-and-gold serenity. Later, in the failing light, a gradual chill sharpening the air. Monks making their slow way back to temples. Children singing folk songs in the dusk. The valley suspended in a virgin silence. "Idyll" was a word from which I was accustomed to recoil, yet truly I felt that there could be nothing lovelier than this peaceful windless valley, so innocent it did not know the meaning of the word. Even in December, it was spring in Paro. And sometimes, walking home through avenues of willows, golden under cobalt skies, I felt as if I had stumbled upon the hidden Arcadia of Heinrich Harrer's *Seven Years in Tibet*. A sequel, perhaps: *Several Weeks in Bhutan*.

The weeks, too, began to take shape as I grew accustomed to Bhutan. On Saturday afternoons, copper-faced men would gather in front of the avenue of willows behind the hotel and there, in the brilliant sunshine, the mountains behind them, send straight arrows shooting through the quiet air. Farther along, beyond the Sportsgrounds, was the peaceable bustle of the weekend market. Boxes of "Power-Packed" Surf, piles of fruit protected from the sun by rusty umbrellas, cows' heads lying on the ground. Photos of orange-robed monks, cartons of "Ready to Eat Cheese Crispies," men banging cymbals in an afternoon sweetened by the scent of tangerines. The heads alone caught all the scene's variety: bowler hats, woolen caps, Yankees baseball hats; cowboy hats, turbans, turquoise-twined plaits; green scarves, pink bows, and bobbled woolen berets.

Weekends were also the time when news came to Thimphu, in the form of *Kuensel*, the two-year-old weekly English-language bulletin. This was a paper rich in surprises. "Yak semen is being imported from Mongolia for the first time," cried the front page. The first page of the World News section was given over to a long article on the thirtieth anniversary of Paddington Bear. The letters column featured a generalized exhortation to "Make a habit of keeping your bowels moving regularly." And one whole page of the twelve-page paper was taken up by an advertisement for Thai Air.

The bowel injunction was not, it seemed, untypical. One week, five different articles on pages 2 and 3 of *Kuensel* addressed the issue of health. A review commended the Chode Junior High School for its fine "health drama." The Dzongda of Paro opined that "Animal health is human wealth." The weekly quiz was devoted to AIDS. And the Leisure Page was, rather surprisingly, dominated by a comic strip with the title "Why Is Tobacco Bad?"

Health was a natural enough concern, of course, in a land where the average life expectancy is only forty-four and where two hundred schoolchildren must sometimes share a single cold-water tap. But the thrust of *Kuensel*'s campaigns was more specific and, in its way, more generalized. "SMOKING," announced the sign at Thimphu bus station. "Buddhist Dharma says smoking is a great sin. Modern science has proved smoking is dangerous to health. Medical science says—Smoking is very bad to your health." In much the same spirit, the Ministry for Social Services presented itself as a "smoke-free zone" and went on to proclaim: "Blessed are those who stopped smoking. More blessed are those who never started it." Even at the turn of the century, I later discovered, official Bhutanese law was fulminating against "a most filthy and noxious herb, tobacco, sure to steep the sacred images and books in pollution and filth" and likely, it was felt, to cause "wars and big epidemics." That it was still harping on the theme almost a hundred years later seemed testimony not only to the constancy but also to the inefficacy of the appeal. Besides, in a country whose king's most famous passion (after basketball) was Havana cigars, the antismoking campaign did not, I thought, have a promising future.

Sometimes, in the afternoon, I ventured inside the inner sanctum of the public library, a kindergarten-size room appointed with a few rickety baby-blue shelves, less than four feet tall, and a couple of worktables, distinguished by a total absence of lights. This last deficiency, given the library's opening hours (1:00–6:00 p.m.), occasionally posed problems. But the patient explorer was amply rewarded for his pains. For the Thimphu Public Library had everything from Woody Allen to Czeslaw Milosz and García Márquez (though, through a quirk of cataloguing, the shelves were labeled not with the categories of books but with the names of donors—thus "IMF" and "World Bank" signs led to *Tender Taming* and *The Magic of Love*, and Barbara Cartland was brought far closer to Barber B. Conable than either might ever have expected). And the staff was full of typical Bhutanese solicitude. When, once, I settled down with Jackie Collins's *Rock Star*, a teenage librarian hurried up to present me with some notepaper.

On days when the library did not satisfy my literary needs, I could always turn to the ever-talkative trash cans, to the city's loquacious bumper stickers (FLOWER IS TO KEEP BUT NOT TO TAKE, advised one epic of gnomic lyricism, GIRLFRIEND IS TO MAKE BUT NOT TO BREAK), or to Bhutanese toilet paper (for in U.N. adviser–crowded Thimphu, even this came wrapped in tubes that muttered, "CCD camera, power supply . . . and reliable platform [version II] . . . with highly integrated . . . graphics software . . . serve the needs . . . C service code"). My most profitable reading, though, came in the volume entitled *Bhutan Telephone Directory 1986 Fire Tiger Year*. This seventy-six-page publication sufficed for the entire country (two pages, in fact, were enough for all the private companies in Thimphu), and many of its pages contained invaluable tips for living. It began, alarmingly, with "Guidelines for Telephone Users" ("Dial carefully to avoid wrong numbers. Speak clearly, not loudly. Please be brief on telephone. Urgent calls may be waiting for you"). It quickly moved on, however, to more recondite material, advising readers that it takes an operator thirty-five seconds to answer for a trunk (i.e., long-distance) call and that "when you dial for booking, you come in queue." Trunk calls, however, came in six categories: Urgent, Lightning, Distress, Important, Immediate, and Most Immediate. But was Urgent faster than Lightning? And why was Immediate the same price as Most Immediate? And what did any of it mean, since a Distress call was treated "same as ordinary call"?

Much of this, in any case, was academic, since only "His Majesty" and "His Holiness" were allowed to make Most Immediate calls ("State Monks" and "Red Scarf Officers" were allowed to make Immediate ones).

And all of it, besides, was based on the highly unlikely eventuality that a call could be placed at all. I tried one trunk call—from Paro to Thimphu, forty miles away—but having dialed carefully to avoid wrong numbers, waited thirty-five seconds, and come in queue, I ended up forced to speak so loudly (but not clearly) that I could probably have been heard in Thimphu without benefit of telephone lines. Local calls within Thimphu were scarely easier, since they had to be booked from my room, and my room was not hooked up to any switchboard. Even if it had been, I would probably not have managed to make a call, since there was only one line in the hotel, and if any of its thirty or so guests was using the phone, the line was used up. Even a call within the hotel was treacherous: every time a caller asked for room service, his shouted requests were broadcast to everyone in the dining room.

Things went wrong every day in Bhutan. Keys fell off chains, doors locked one in, taps refused to turn. Twice in twenty minutes one night, the lights went off, and then again as I was busy flooding my bathroom. The reception desk at the Olathang Hotel—though there were less than a dozen guests in its fifty-six rooms—was littered with a pile of sad pink slips: "Room 411 No Hot Water." "Room 423. No Electricity. No Water." "Room 417 . . ." One night I awoke with a start at 4:15 a.m. to see the puny heater that was the only thing standing between me and frostbite spitting out white sparks, hissing like a snake, and then, with a magician's flamboyant puff, exploding into oblivion.

Yet what was most surprising about Bhutan was how little, really, went wrong, how efficiently everything worked. Like the other countries of the High Himalayas, Bhutan had an air of gentleness and calm that left no room for chaos. And the Bhutanese I met were unfailingly punctual and unreasonably honest. Their voices were soft and measured, in the dignified Himalayan way, resonant with a sense of energy contained. And what impressed me most, the longer I stayed, was not so much that the people did not know foreign goods as that they did not seem to want to know them. Theirs seemed a genuine innocence, the result of choice as much as circumstance, in a protected land where schoolboys told me that their favorite parties were the ones that featured "monk dances." All the time I was in Bhutan, nobody ever asked me for a favor or troubled me with an outstretched hand; the Bhutanese people hardly seemed interested in me—as a foreigner—at all. Again and again I had occasion to recall that the ever informative *Olympic Villager* in Seoul had declared that of all the 160 teams at the games, the Bhutanese was the most polite. The little girls who greeted me along the road sang out, "Good afternoon, sir," and followed it up with a graceful bow; even the soldier who, quite rightly, evicted me from Tonga Dzong was all courtesy and apologies.

At the same time, however, I suspected that this flawless politeness was also a way of keeping foreigners at a distance. Part of the local reticence arose, I thought, from a shyness that was utterly engaging, and part of it from an unfeigned sense of cultural dignity and pride that was genuinely moving. But there was also a wariness, a watchfulness in the people, as strong as in their impenetrable dzongs. And the dzongs themselves struck me always as strategic more than spiritual establishments; as fortifications rather than golden palaces or monasteries. Bhutan had the red-robed monks, the butter lamps, the chants, the scriptures, the prayer halls, and the faces of Tibet, but it had none of that country's fire and intensity, none of its radiant magnetism. Bhutan may have got its name from the Sanskrit *Bhotanta*, or the east end of Tibet. Yet it seemed in many ways a near inversion of Tibet. And where in Tibet the air fairly vibrates with the strength of religious devotion, Bhutan struck me as a strangely secular place.

This sense of self-enclosure, the sense that people and buildings were always keeping an eye on one—Bhutan had little of the instant friendliness of much of Asia, just as it had none of its importunacy or intrusiveness—clearly matched the institutionalized suspiciousness of the government itself. Even in hotels, Bhutanese doors were guarded as tightly as those of any Manhattan apartment, with padlocks under double bolts. And the country's great fear—of being overrun by tourists, being "Nepalmed," in a sense—was not, of course, without foundation. Nepal, after all, had hardly opened its doors to the world before it was being colonized as the ultimate hippie outpost, Shangri-la on two dollars a day; in the twenty years since, temples had been disfigured, the people's respect for temples had been deformed, and most incredibly of all, per capita income had actually fallen. "There is a perception abroad that we are trying to discourage tourism," a top Bhutanese official told me over tea one day. "That is not true. We want to encourage it. But we want tourists in the package form. Look at Nepal. There are people there who are dirty, with long hair and bad clothes. Women who will have sex with anyone. Pot, marijuana. People sleeping in the streets." His voice picked up heat as he thought of the countercultural Gomorrah. "This we do not want in Bhutan."

As he continued his tirade, with impassioned defensiveness, I began to detect another strain that had grown more apparent to me the longer I spent in the country: the fact that the government is more than ready to make all the people's decisions for them. "We are officially a constitutional monarchy," this high-ranking official told me, "but really we are a democratic monarchy—a democracy with a king. One hundred of the one hundred fifty members of our National Assembly are democratically elected. Eight of our ten-man Royal Advisory Council are chosen." What he neglected to say—protesting so much—was that the majority of the voters, and even the candidates they chose, were illiterate; that none of the advisers wanted, or was likely, to go against the king; that in many respects Bhutan is still in a state of benevolent despotism. The government provides all its people with free education and health care; in return, however, it feels free to make certain demands of them. All buildings must be constructed in the traditional style. No school trips may be taken out of the country. No Bhutanese may hold foreign currency. No Bhutanese may study abroad—unless he is sponsored by the government. If he is sponsored, he must sign a pact promising to return to serve the country. And when he returns, he must go through a reeducation program to remind him of his heritage. Christian churches are banned in Bhutan. A foreign woman who marries a Bhutanese man must wait fifteen years to gain Bhutanese citizenship. A Bhutanese woman who marries a foreign man immediately loses all her rights. The Bhutanese love their country—and just in case they don't, the government reminds them that they must.

I met only one person in Bhutan who felt bold enough to discuss this feudal legacy with me, a government official of unusual eloquence. The most disturbing thing about the situation, he said, was not that the government made the people's minds up for them but rather that the people seemed to want it so. Released from serfdom only thirty years before, the masses still seemed happy to have their civil servants do their living for them. And the government did everything possible to encourage this dependency, even going so far as to provide "Etiquette Training" for government officials to remind them that they must, when meeting the king, perform a full three-part prostration, as if in the presence of a temple.

The same kind of anxious authoritarianism was evident, I felt, in the government's handling of the outside world. Bhutan, of course, has a long and distinguished tradition of standoffishness. As early as 1838, officers of the never-colonized country were bastinadoing residents who got too close to foreigners; and when the British threatened the Bhutanese with vengeance (for whisking off cattle, and sometimes British subjects, from across the border), the Dragon Ruler responded by simply threatening the British with a divine force of twelve angry gods, who were, he added, "very ferocious ghosts."

(Some of this, no doubt, must be taken with a pinch of salt—or barley meal, at least. When Sir Ashley Eden pronounced the Bhutanese to be "immoral and indecent in their habits to an extent which almost surpassed belief," he may have been airing a largely private grievance. According to a British clergyman, writing in the July 1898 *Calcutta Review*, in the course of Sir Ashley's 1863 visit, one Bhutanese "took a large piece of wet barley meal out of his tea-cup and, with a roar of laughter, rubbed the paste all about Mr. Eden's face. He then pulled his hair, slapped him on the back, and indulged in several disagreeable practical jokes.")

Yet even allowing for peeved exaggeration, Bhutan had long shown a singular gift for keeping the world at arm's length. And even now, with great civility and customary efficiency, the Bhutanese had foreigners exactly where they wanted them: the foreign advisers were accommodated in the twenty-dollar-a-night hotels downtown, while tourists "in the package form" were sequestered in remote hilltop hotels, an hour's walk from the locals, paying $250 a night. Protecting the country's culture was one reason for continuing the policy. But there seemed to be another. For by now, Bhutan's cachet lies primarily in its remoteness: people want to visit it precisely because most people cannot visit it. Bhutan is a beautiful and peaceful and magical land, but so, too, are many of the areas around the Himalayas; and those who want to explore the mountains can do so with more convenience and comfort, at literally one-tenth the price, in Nepal, while those who are drawn to Tibetan Buddhism can now go straight to the source—Tibet—or to the high lunar spaces of Ladakh. What attracts foreigners to Bhutan is mostly the fact that, as the travel brochure says, it is "one of the most exclusive and rare destinations for any tourist." And Bhutan guards its chastity with an iron lock. If the Hidden Kingdom were to open up to the world, there might be not only cultural but economic loss.

In recent years, however, the pressure on the isolated kingdom has begun to build. The Dalai Lama describes how twenty-eight Tibetans living in Bhutan were suddenly arrested, tortured, and thrown without trial into jail. And recently, when the Dragon Ruler issued his latest edict ordering all Bhutanese citizens to wear traditional dress while in public—and, in the same breath, expelling every immigrant who had arrived since 1958—the roughly 400,000 Nepalis who represent almost a quarter of the population rose up in protest, stripping Bhutanese civilians of their clothes and calling out for democracy, until they were violently put down. Even in the course of my own stay, I could sense the first stirrings of a modernizing impulse. The new jet was one sign of this, and there was already talk of an airport terminal that would hold 160 people. One afternoon I wandered out of the Druk Hotel to watch the archers in the Sportsgrounds, and returned less than an hour later to find the nation's first American Express stickers proudly plastered to the door. The country had even just completed its first feature-length movie, a $6,500 spectacular about a star-crossed couple: she dies, he throws himself on the funeral pyre, and both live happily ever after as an ox and a cow.

Yet what I remember best about Bhutan seems unlikely to change very soon. What I remember best is sipping chilled mango juice in the sunlit mornings and walking through blue afternoons, silent save for the snapping of prayer flags; or climbing up mountains to the whitewashed monasteries and watching the lights come on in the valleys below. When, on my last day in Bhutan, I returned to the Thimphu library, to cancel my membership there, one of the young librarians hurried up to greet me. "Just now you go to America, sir?" Yes. "How long to America, sir?" Maybe two days. "Oh, sir! America is very far from Bhutan! Here in Bhutan, sir, we cannot imagine America!" The same, I thought, was more than true in reverse.

In Hue, the gracious, reticent capital of old Vietnam, I drifted one morning, by sampan, down to the Linh Mu pagoda, its gardens scented with orchids, frangipani, and jackfruit, and scattered with a flutter of white and crimson butterflies. Monks with girlish faces ushered me into the kitchen, where eleven-year-old novices, tassel-haired, were slicing vegetables and stoking fires. Then, over tea and green-bean cake, the head abbot, smiling-eyed, told me about how Buddhism had long been suppressed in his country, and pointed out to me the grayish Austin, sitting neatly in the temple garden, in which a monk from the pagoda had driven to Saigon to immolate himself in 1963. Later that day, I walked around the lakeside pavilions where the emperor Tu Duc had once composed poems, sipped lotus tea, and dallied with his 104 courtesans; I wandered into the shaded, pink-walled French colonial school where Ho Chi Minh, General Vo Nguyen Giap, and former Prime Minister Ngo Dinh Diem had all been educated (and, as ever in Hue, felt as if I were walking through an avenue of smiles); and that night, I returned to the kind of lyric pleasures I had come to expect in Vietnam—the couples gathered in cafés along the waterside, sitting on wicker chairs, their glasses balanced on stones, and watching the lights on the river while a syrupy

female singer softened the night. (Nearby, others were lined
up in rows on chairs, entranced by a video advertised by hand-
painted signs of an Oriental-featured Meryl Streep, with "Os-
car-winner" written in Vietnamese.) In Hue, watching the famous local beauties, flowerlike in their traditional ao dais,
pedaling, with queenly serenity, across the Perfume River, long
hair falling to their waists and pink parasols held up against the
sun, I felt that here was a scene that could move even a journalist
to poetry. Just one week later, to my astonishment, I read, in
Morley Safer's *Flashbacks,* that even this most hardheaded of
investigative journalists had, he confessed, written a poem in
Hue—which "mercifully, [he had] both lost and forgotten."

A few days later, I was inside the busiest and brashest circus
I had ever seen. Saigon could be called Scooter City, the home
of the Motorcycle Revolution, a 350 cc Beijing. For every weekend night, all the golden youth of town dress up in their Sunday
best, get onto their bikes, and start racing and roaring around
the central streets, swerving in and out of packs, speeding along
in swarms, girls in cocktail dresses, boys in white shirts and
ties, whole families on a single scooter, teenagers in denim
skirts, even demure old gray-haired couples, all of them roaring
around and around and around, past high-rise murals that say
TO KEEP MONEY IN THE BANK IS PATRIOTIC, past packs of others
lined up along the sidewalks, the whole group of them enacting
a kind of crazy, revved-up *thé dansant* on wheels. The feverish
carnival atmosphere was like nothing I had ever known before:
in Italian towns, teenagers famously promenade around the
main plaza in the evenings, exchanging glances and flirtations,
but here the whole ritual was speeded up, intensified, and
played out at top volume, half of Saigon caught up in this
surging mass, trading smiles as they went, catching the eyes of
strangers, or simply exulting in a literal version of their brand-
new motto of *song voi,* or "living fast." It seemed an almost

perfect metaphor for the sudden explosion of energy and excitement in Saigon, as sharp as if a rubber band, stretched out for fifteen years, had suddenly snapped back, and with a vengeance. And as the night wore on, the feverish sense of abandon grew ever more surreal: somehow, in Saigon, it is always nine-thirty at night in some flashy, shady dive, and a chanteuse in a sequined microskirt is belting out "I'm on top of the world, looking down on creation . . ." to the accompaniment of violins and cellos played by girls in shocking-pink miniskirts.

Vietnam, to me, seemed two distinct, almost contradictory countries: Saigon (Ho Chi Minh City) and the rest. And each, in a sense, is a refutation of the other. In part, of course, this reflects nothing more than the universal disjunction between big city and unspoiled countryside, equally apparent around New York, Paris, Buenos Aires, and Bangkok. In part, it reflects merely the geography of a country that was divided in half two decades ago, and two centuries: Hanoi is as far north of Ho Chi Minh City as Boston is of Charleston, and the character, the pace, even the climate of the quiet, unshowy, northern capital bear little relation to the helter-skelter, anything-goes vitality of the south (in ten days in the north, I never saw the sun; in ten days in the south, I almost got charbroiled). Even now, as South Vietnam completes what some are calling a "reverse reunification," the two aspects of the country are as different as past and future, silence and frenzy, maiden aunt and bargirl—as different, ultimately, as Beijing and Hong Kong. Ask someone in Hanoi if she's ever been to Saigon, and she'll say, "No, I've never been outside Vietnam." Her cousin in the south will say the opposite. Saigon and Vietnam are as different, almost literally, as night and day.

Yet both places are distinctly new to foreign eyes, and both paces—that of an aging bicycle and that of a juiced-up Honda—have their own exhilarations. It is hard, in fact, not to grow woozily romantic when enumerating the holiday seductions of the place: there are the mist-wreathed rain forests of the west and north, where you can find fifty-three distinct minority tribes—each with its own colorful costume, customs, and tongue—hunting, still, with bows and arrows and, if asked how old they are, answering "ten or fifteen water buffalos' lives." There are the atmospheric old French villas and hotels, peeling behind coconut palms and green gates, made more nostalgic now by decay and lined up along avenues of tamarind. There are the exquisite temples and remains of the fourteenth-century Cham civilization, as "brilliant and neurotic," in Norman Lewis's well-chosen words, as those of the Khmer in Cambodia next door. There are the illuminated lanterns and oil-lit lamps along the crooked streets at night, which take you back to the Indochina of your dreams (or of Tintin books), and there are the urbane pleasures of white-linen restaurants serving mandarin juice and coq au vin while serenading you with piano-and-violin duets. There are 1,400 miles of coastline studded with pure-white deserted beaches, and there are prices that are extravagantly low (136 huge reproductions of masterpieces from the Hermitage Museum in Saint Petersburg can be had for one dollar, and a tube of lipstick for ten cents). Most of all, though, there are the exceptionally attractive, cultured, and hospitable people, still so unused to foreigners that they light up at the sight, yet self-possessed, too, and full of the quick intelligence for which they have long been famous. "The Vietnamese are the last natural human people in the world," a well-traveled Korean businessman told me, a little hyperbolically, perhaps, over drinks in Hanoi, in between discussing the relative merits of Highway 5 and the 101 freeway in California.

Yet the real attraction of Vietnam today is something deeper. When we choose a place to visit, the way a country carries itself and markets itself—the way it knows itself, really—is

everything. We flee certain resorts not just because they are
touristed but more because they have begun to see themselves
through tourists' eyes, to amend themselves to tourists' needs,
to carry themselves in capital letters: because, in short, they
have simplified themselves into their sense of what a foreigner
wants. Thus even a country as irresistible and various as Thailand is beginning to feel used up, exhausted and eroded by the
six million visitors who pass through each year, and losing a
little of its soul with each transaction. Thailand—like Cancún,
or the Lake District, or many of the lovely places of the world—
seems to have mastered the art of selling itself while giving
almost nothing of itself away.

None of this is true—yet—of Vietnam, which still has the
bashful charm of a naturally alluring girl stepping out into bright
sunlight after years of dark seclusion. Protected, ironically, by
its years of hardship and cut off from modernity by more than
a decade of Communist rule, Vietnam is still, more than most
places, new to the world. It does not know what to make of us,
nor we of it. Its pleasures feel unrehearsed, and surprise is still
a growth industry.

That is one reason, of course, why everyone seems to be
converging on it—Bangkok-based stockbrokers, Japanese businessmen, budget travelers from Europe—all eager to grab a
piece of the hidden treasure before it splinters or corrodes.
Vietnam has very much the feel of the coming thing, the next
"little dragon," tomorrow's hot destination: a perfect locale,
indeed, for the kinder, greener, post–cold war nineties. And it
is already beginning to become a crossroads of the fashionable:
in my hotel in Hanoi, an assistant producer from Paradis Films
was bargaining over a suite for Mme. Deneuve (acting in one
of the three feature-length French motion pictures being shot
in the country at the time); when I went to the Cao Dai church
in Tay Ninh, the name above mine in the visitors' book was that

of Gough Whitlam, former prime minister of Australia. And one night in Saigon, walking through a street so crowded one could hardly move, I bumped, quite literally, into two colleagues from New York.

All this is also the reason why Vietnam is changing before one's very eyes—and anyone who saw Bangkok or Beijing five years ago and revisits them today knows that these Eastern cities can take off with the urgency of a Chinese firecracker. Ever since the government in Hanoi decided to open up the country to free trade and private enterprise in 1987, the famous energy and enterprise of the Vietnamese have been transforming the country overnight (three years ago, by all accounts, there was scarcely a motorbike in Saigon). And already, compromise is beginning to appear and some of the village innocence to fade. Already, you can feel that shy glances and modest giggles may soon be a thing of the past; already, four-color brochures, and even AIDS, may be just around the corner. Vietnam is developing at the speed of a Polaroid. At present, the country is held back mostly by Washington's sixteen-year-old trade embargo, which makes it difficult for Hanoi to receive IMF and World Bank loans, severely limits its trade opportunities, and leaves the hardworking Vietnamese literally all dressed up with no place to go (save round and round the center of Saigon). But as soon as the conditions change, the country is ready to take off, and already the sense of boomtown electricity is almost palpable: as if much of the country were letting out its breath, in a great gust of exhalation, after years of holding it in.

For the moment, though, the country's facilities are still, thankfully, uncertain. Some hotels in Vietnam offer elevators, some have watercoolers, some have girls who slip into your room the minute you return from dinner. Some have Viettronics shortwave radios in each room, some high-tech phones so complex they cannot reach even the front desk, some caged monkeys inexplicably in their gardens. In one deluxe hotel I stayed in, keys were scattered across the reception desk so that any guest could effectively take the key to any room (communal property indeed!). In another, ubiquitous signs warned: PETS, FIRE ARMS, EXPLOSIVES, INFLAMABLES, AND STINKING THINGS ARE NOT ALLOWED IN THE HOTEL. In another, I went into my room one day to find a chambermaid cadging a free shower. Vietnam is still the kind of place where you look out of your hotel window to see not two, not three, but nine cows grazing on the lawn.

Vietnam is also the kind of place where restaurants offer armadillo, and cobras that are slaughtered at your table; artichoke tea, gecko-steeped liqueurs, and—the specialty of Dalat—coffee made from beans vomited up by a weasel. It is a place where beer costs more than wine, and a Coke sets you back more than an entire meal. When once I ordered filet mignon and french fries, my waiter graciously apologized for being slow—but french fries, he explained, were very hard to cook.

Vietnam is also a place where traveling by car means bumping along Highway 1, through a confusion of bicycles shrouded in brushes and brooms, buses piled high with tail-wagging dogs, and horse-drawn carts, at speeds no faster than 10 mph, over "elephant holes" that put out the backs of any foreigners who are not banging their heads against the roof, and where, after nightfall, the only lights one sees are reflections in the eyes of passing water buffalos. The alternative—taking the local airline—may not be any happier. On the flight I took, all the seats on the back two rows were different colors, the portholes were guarded by flimsy curtains, and the back third of this former Soviet military plane was an empty space with trays of meatballs stacked on the floor (and later handed out by a phlegmatic teenage boy). The whole place had the air of a hospital waiting room in the clouds.

That kind of erratic infrastructure has, so far, helped to keep Vietnam relatively untouristed: 1990 was the "Year of Tourism," my guide in the north dryly informed me, and it was also the year when the government decided to tear down all its hotels (in order to rebuild them). As a result, the country attracted exactly 187,000 visitors, or one for every twenty-five who went to smaller Thailand, next door. And the sightseer with even minimal expectations of comfort and ease may still find Vietnam more than he has bargained for: the spirit is winning, but the flush is weak. For the jaded traveler, however, who has begun to despair of ever finding anywhere fresh or unspoiled, the place may well be a revelation. Vietnam is amazingly short of amenities, but one goes to Vietnam today precisely to enjoy the qualities that the absence of such amenities encourages.

The only preparation you need to make if you plan to visit Vietnam is to sweep your mind clear of all preconceptions. To begin with, Americans need fear nothing except an excess of curiosity and goodwill, and the insults of children who mistake them for Soviets; these days, much of Vietnam is praying for a greater American presence. As for the Vietnamese army, though it is the fifth-largest in the world, the only sign I saw of it in all my time in the country was in the fifteen honeymoon cottages it rents out in Dalat, the "City of Love." And the Socialist Republic of Vietnam is also one of the least ideological, or Marxist-minded, places I have ever seen, buzzing as it does with an enterprise that could not be freer, and principles mostly honored in the breach. In three weeks in the country, I saw almost no slogans, no billboards, no assertions of any principle save for a generalized veneration of Ho Chi Minh (whose poster you can buy for three cents, framed for thirty) and his relatively anodyne saying "Nothing is more precious than freedom and

independence." And where in Cuba, say, or North Korea, police seem to be a part of every conversation and everyone is
always looking over his shoulder, the Vietnamese I met seemed
more than ready to air their grievances in the street. It is ironic
that so many of us associate Vietnam with hardship and war; I
found it one of the gentlest and most peaceful countries I have
ever seen.

The wonkiness of Vietnam won me over as soon as I set foot in
Hanoi: its tiny airport packed with dilapidated old warplanes
and the weathered jets of Balkan Airlines and CSA; the local
passengers filing out with "Operation Smile" buttons on their
lapels; the small figures waving to us from the "See-Off Area."
Inside, the bare shed of an Arrivals Hall was flooded with manic
French dance tunes played at top volume. Stick figures on slips
of paper denoted the male and female rest rooms, and pretty
customs officers seemed mostly to be inspecting foreigners for
smiles. Outside, a few dutiful drivers were stroking their Toyo-
tas with pink feather dusters.

Our car set off along the half-paved roads, past men on motorbikes in shades and army caps, their women riding sidesaddle
behind them, past blasted, wheezing buses. "The last time I
was here," offered the Thai businessman who was along for the
ride, "my friend's room caught on fire: something to do with
the air conditioner. I tried to find a bellboy or waiter to help,
but the only way I could explain to them what was happening
was by putting on my lighter. When I did, they offered me a
cigarette. It was a very good experience somehow!"

Hanoi at first sight felt like a small town writ large, the ancient
thirty-six-street capital pushed out just a little but touched still
with a sleepy, leafy elegance. High-school girls skipped rope
along the main boulevard, and boys banged rusted Foosball sets
across the sidewalk. Students cycled hand in hand down the

busy streets. Around the central lake, Hoan Kiem, old men sat fishing, while others gathered over games of Chinese chess; in Indira Gandhi Park, teenage boys with inch-long thumbnails and twigs like studs in their ears crouched above the ground, playing cards. Outside the former U.S. embassy, boys were playing *takraw* (foot volleyball), using a flower as a ball.

Hanoi felt utterly authentic, very much itself and not a user-friendly replica of itself, let alone a Communist-planned Potemkin antiself: the only sign of Tourism was the name on the packs of local cigarettes. Yet even here, amidst this virgin quiet, one could feel a steady buzz of restless, mercantile energy. Along the tree-lined streets, pretty with shuttered consulates and overgrown old villas, there was still a furious commotion of *cyclos*, bicycles, and pedestrians, so crowded that a car could hardly pass; and along the age-old, sloping streets, a dizzying seethe of shops and stalls. In days gone by, the streets of the old quarter were called Cotton and Silk and Comb, each one offering a single commodity; today the names remain, but one street is devoted to motorbikes and one to Sony Walkmans; one has nothing but Seiko watches, one only fake bank notes, to be offered to the dead.

Insofar as any Marxism is to be found in Vietnam, Hanoi, of course, is the place, yet even in the capital it is hardly strident or insistent. A statue of "Le-nin" stands forlornly in one park, and a vast open space surrounds one of the few new buildings in town, the Ho Chi Minh Mausoleum, an eerily illuminated chamber, guarded by ramrod soldiers, which sightseers can visit only with a white-gloved military escort. "Ho Chi Minh would have hated it," said my guide. The Cuban-built Thang Loi Hotel has all the standard Cuban amenities (no water in the swimming pool, no staff at the counters), and at night, in the bar, I watched beefy Russians toasting one another tearily over thirty-cent bottles of vodka and negotiating for the night with local girls. Groups of peasants from the countryside troop all day long around the Ho Chi Minh Museum, but the main subject of interest for them may well be the corner that features a Coke sign, a plaster-cast Packard, and Don McCullin's photo of a shell-shocked grunt. Outside the house of Uncle Ho, former pastry chef at London's Carlton Hotel, they were selling copies of *Totto-chan*, the memoirs of Japan's female Johnny Carson.

For most of the people in Hanoi, with their cash-register quickness and low-key patriotism, there are more urgent concerns than ideology. My guide to the city, a friendly, cherubic fellow in a baseball cap, with a ready grin, had been a Vietcong platoon commander for four years, but even his accounts of the war were matter-of-fact and hardly partisan. His greatest challenge, he implied, had come when he was sent, as soon as the war ended, to Bulgaria and, on his second day there, after four years of fighting in the jungle, had been told by an eighteen-year-old Bulgarian girl, "I love you." He also seemed cheerfully unillusioned about the system. Had Bulgarian served him well in his job? "In eleven years," he said, "there have been only two Bulgarian tour groups in Vietnam. I was assigned to neither." The present moment, with its promise of economic openness and its freedom from strife, was the sunniest period in his forty years, he said. But still he started every sentence with "The problem is that . . ." and, on the rare occasions when he tried to make a political point, somehow got the words all wrong. "During the war, the North Vietnamese were very barbarous—I mean, courageous. . . ."

Besides, the nominal principles of the Party are contradicted all day long by a cacophony of deals. Everywhere seems a marketplace in Hanoi, and every street is bubbling over with free trade: one block given over to a stack of black-and-white TVs, one to a rack of bicycles. In another block, thirty barbers were lined up with their backs to traffic, their mirrors set along the wall before them. Old men puffed Hero and Gallantes cigarettes over pyramids of Nescafé bottles, bookshops exploded with stacks of Madonna fan mags, copies of *Ba Tuoc Mongto Crixto* (and, of course, piles of TOEFL Preparation Books). In the covered market, fifteen-dollar-a-kilo turtles and fat snakes sat next to MARADONA JEANS caps and shirts with ONE HUNDRED DOLLARS on them. And out on the streets, the stalls were loaded with knockoff Casios, Disney T-shirts, Hong Kong watches, Chinese fans, Snoopy bags, flashing clocks, and pills guaranteed to save one from "addiction to narcotics." An absence of external resources is more than made up for by inner: a teacher in Vietnam earns nine dollars a month, yet half the households in the country, according to my guide, have VCRs.

In Hanoi, I soon learned to do as the Vietnamese do: hope for the best. A taxi ride into town, I learned, might mean a motorbike race, clinging to the back of a young soldier; laundry service meant flinging your clothes upon a bed and hoping you might see them sometime later. Prices varied wildly, and inexplicably, from one place to the next, with some articles costing eight or twelve times more in one place than another. Hanoi had certainly not resolved itself into the International Style.

And nighttime was the best of all in the old, and stately, capital, as something ancient began to come forth from the shadows. I loved to bump along the lamplit alleyways after dark in a *cyclo*, a perfect pace at which to see and smell the spicy nights. In the gloom, the town was more mysterious than ever, the streets too dark even to read by, the little stalls half lit, the faces eerie in the blackness. Lovers were eating ice cream by the waterside, and children traded cards of movie stars. Whole families sat at tables on the sidewalk, eating elaborate meals by the flicker of oil lamps. Couples sat cradled by their bicycles, or in the hollows of large trees. The air smelled of mint and a festival spirit. And it was easy to feel that lamps were burning inside the people too.

In Hanoi, I came to see how much the Vietnamese are still a people of simple, romantic pleasures, making do with what they have: playing badminton on the streets, or going for walks along the lake, or simply taking in the softness of the night air. Gambling and photography are still as popular as in Norman Lewis's lyrical accounts from the fifties; and soft-laughing girls still promenade around the lake at night. In stores I entered, owners offered me tea and lotus-seed cake; in the distance, Johnny Guitar was playing "Romance d'Amour."

Of course, Hanoi is changing with every passing season. Along Hang Ga Street, more and more places now are sprouting the magic word, in English, "restaurant" (and offering cognac and Cyndi Lauper, though their menus still have sections headed "River Tortoises" or, simply, "Birds"), and proprietors are more and more likely to invite you inside to see their lambada videos or discuss Samantha Fox. The famous mantra "Eric Clapton Number One" can often be heard in Hanoi now, and along the candlelit streets at night, crowds can be seen in houses, lined up in rows as at a cinema, their faces lit up by a new Nintendo screen. On page 4 of the local paper, *Hanoi Moi*, I found a discussion of *Pretty Woman*. Yet still there is an unhardened sweetness to the place, an innocence of the pleasures it is giving.

In the countryside, the changes are even more pronounced. Brand-new brick houses are popping up in every village, TVs are lighting up the dark, scooters are closing in on water buffalo. Every other child seems to be wearing a baseball cap that announces, enigmatically, THE RATS WON. And yet, and yet, there is a real sense of unexpectedness on the road, as one slices through the clouded mountains in the north, around a series of narrow switchbacks, the only figures materializing in the mist the tribal Montagnards, clad in their red and blue and yellow scarves and belts. We stopped for lunch at a tiny hut, eating, cross-legged on a platform, the standard street-stall fare of beef and pork lit up by mint and lemongrass; in the distance, ridge after ridge of dark-blue mountains receded into outline, the same color, almost, as the teeth of the tribal crone who served us tea. The minority Montagnards still measure their lives by the essential village rhythm of cockcrow and chopping wood. Exquisite, swan-necked beauties, jangling silver bracelets, draw water from the well or work old rice pumps with their feet; others go down to the water to bathe, and chatter away in classic, antique Thai. As visitors increase, the tribal peoples are beginning to learn how to play themselves (the altar in one hut I saw contained a bottle of Johnnie Walker Red, a can of 7-Up, and a packet of Gitanes), but they are still at least five years behind their more photographed cousins across the border.

The single most beautiful sight in all Vietnam may well be Halong Bay, five hours south of Hanoi—a local version of China's Guilin—its waters dotted with three thousand misty islets in the shape of tigers, unicorns, and fighting cocks. On the day I visited, it was rainy, and I spent most of the afternoon wandering around the deserted colonnades and lazy balconies of a French colonial hotel I had entirely to myself. Yet, despite the rain, one could still make out the watercolor beauty of the area, billow-sailed junks outlined against jagged outcrops, kingfishers skimming low above the water. In the early light, fishermen casting nets glided silent across the silent water.

Like most tropical countries, Vietnam gets up with the light, and one of the greatest pleasures you can find is to go outside at six in the morning and see the whole town out stretching its limbs, playing badminton or soccer in the streets, ghosting its way through tai chi motions. When fishing boats go out at midday, fireworks herald their good fortune. And at night, ev-

eryone heads for the water again, assembling at video cafés that
sometimes offer "300-inch screens" (or Richard Chamberlain
miniseries doing battle against kung fu classics).

It was gray and rainy every morning I was in the north, yet
every morning, as I looked up at the sky, someone would assure
me, "A very propitious day. In Vietnam, the rainy season lasts
from September to January." It was now mid-April. "This is
the best season of the year." Yet the gray only intensified the
country's matchless greens. All of us probably know by heart
the classic landscape of Vietnam: the tiny stick figures in lamp-
shade hats silhouetted on the hilltops, the quilted emerald rice
fields, the slow-moving, pendulous water buffalo. Village girls
still carry water in two-handled buckets, and men sell rice
packed in banana leaves along the streets. And the streets themselves are a crazy gallimaufry of unlikely props: Japanese buses
from the Kansai countryside and creaking De Sotos, Minsk
motorbikes and carts loaded with rattan, Peugeot bicycles and
ancient GMC trucks, "moving kitchens" and cross-country
buses that break down only once every forty minutes. Wherever
I went, 95 percent of the people I passed would stare at me, 75
percent would try out "Hello! Where you come from?" and 60
percent would break into the most radiant of smiles.

Yet the real center of yin in Vietnam, as New Agers (or old
mandarins) would say, is Hue, which, like all university towns,
moves to a bicycle rhythm. For many of us, the name most
instantly connotes bombardment, and the savageries of the Tet
offensive; but the nineteenth-century capital of regal pavilions
has never lost its air of gracious reserve and a faded glamour as
picturesque as that of the black-and-white shots of local Lana
Turners pouting down from every streetside Photo Shop. At
one riverside pagoda, a head monk unfurled for me the banned
Buddhist flag, talking all the while of Hermann Hesse and
Krishnamurti. The students on their bicycles carried them-

selves like ancient porcelain. And my guide in Hue, a soft-spoken, scholarly man in spectacles, talked warmly of Tagore. Had he been here during the Tet offensive, I asked. "Yes," he replied quietly. "My mother was killed by a bomb. I was still quite young." But there was no melodrama in his voice, and no self-pity: the people I met seemed much too dignified to dwell on onetime sufferings.

The shadows cast by the war grew deeper as we drove along the spectacular "Pass of Clouds," high above the golden beaches, to Da Nang. Though now it feels like an industrial city, this onetime fishing village is still graced with two extraordinary sights. The first is its Cham Museum, whose lovely, delicate statues of *apsaras* (or angels) and of Hindu deities, as well as of Lord Buddha, evoke the sinuous, curling beauty of a culture of proud aesthetes. The second sight is even more astonishing. We drove out of what was once called "Rocket City," past the abandoned Quonset huts, past the huge American airfield, past land laid waste by Agent Orange, and past the airport, blasted now with Soviet rock 'n' roll. Then, getting out, we climbed up the Marble Mountains, steep hillsides scattered with Buddhist shrines and huge caverns, lit up by sticks of incense and haunted by the looming shadows of twenty-foot Buddhas and Goddesses of Compassion. At the base of one hill is "China Beach," the celebrated R and R center featured in series and song. For years, even as Americans reclined on the sand, their enemy, unbeknownst to the GIs, were five minutes away, licking their wounds in the god-filled caves and shadowing the Yanks' every movement.

Yet for all the freshness of such memories, and for all the bullet holes that scar the mountain, the foreigner has only to say he's from America, and he is greeted with shiningly genuine smiles. "For us, French is the language of power and love," a Vietnamese friend explained. "English is the language of commerce. Russian is the language of quarrels." There are, of course, some practical reasons why Vietnam is so eager to be friendly with America. Every time I changed a traveler's check, the stack of dong I received in return was equivalent to a whole month's wages for most of the locals who would gather round in a circle. Once, in Nha Trang, a woman came up to me and asked, in fluent English, why I didn't simply deliver my postcards by hand after I got back home. It was more fun, I said, to send them from here. "But so expensive," she replied. Chastened, I realized that the ten dollars I was spending on stamps was equal to her salary for a month.

Central Vietnam has always been a kind of shadowy no-man's-land, not quite North Vietnam and not quite South, and liable to go either way. Today these mongrel influences make for a kind of homemade surrealism. In Hue one night, in a deserted French villa where backpackers stay, and chat over five-course dinners each night, a half-black kid came out and motioned for a cigarette. In the background, "In-a-Gadda-da-Vida" was floating through the night. Other aromatic French villas now advertise their versatile attractions: "Telex Coffee Dancing Massage." In Da Nang, the hot item at the local theater was the Originals, a four-piece all-girl Soviet rock 'n' roll band—*glasnost* on eight legs—accompanied by four scantily clad dancers performing post-Madonna dance routines ("like *Henry and June*," remarked one astonished spectator). And as we drove through a smiling village pastoral one day, my guide slipped in the only tape he owned, and suddenly, amidst the huts and rice paddies, lined now with neat white graves, Willie Nelson was singing duets with Merle Haggard and George Jones.

"Adversity breeds wisdom," my idiom-happy guide assured me. "Life's no bed of roses." He had translated the book of *Born on the Fourth of July* into his native tongue, he went on, and he was much concerned with "post-traumatic stress disorder." He talked about Gorbachev's struggles and the greenhouse effect, Rushdie's conversion to Islam and the death of Graham Greene. "But I'm not going to nickel and dime you to death," he concluded, reassuringly.

The most haunting reminder of the war for me, though, was seventy-five miles south of Da Nang. We turned left off the main highway and bounced along a quiet dirt road, bordered on both sides by tall stalks of maize and by children waving at the passing car. It was hard to believe that this quiet village of flowers and wide-eyed toddlers had once seen rivers of blood eight inches deep. Wisps of white floated along the ground from overhanging cotton trees, birds sang from the branches, water buffalo padded through their ageless cycle. But there was also a quiet monument in My Lai, and a few small graves, and a museum in which are preserved the memories of all 504 people who, according to the Vietnamese, were slaughtered on a single morning.

The woman who tends to the memorial pointed out the skinny coconut palm that was, she said, the only witness of the massacre. I asked her where she had been that morning. "I was eleven years old then," she said softly. "I lived a few kilometers away. I saw the helicopters, I heard the explosions. I saw the fires burning. My aunt was killed that day." No less affecting are the comments in the visitors' book that she showed me over tea in the flower-bordered guesthouse: agonized apologies, most of them, from returning GIs, who often wrote simply, "I have no words." My Lai is one of those places, like Hiroshima, that raise difficult questions about peace and truth, and make one quiet when one leaves.

The very quality of the air seems to change as one drives south. The sun comes out, the shadows lengthen, and the coconut palms begin to multiply. Here one is indisputably in tropical country. And as the visitor approaches Saigon, Saigon comes up to greet him: words of English begin to appear, little kids sprout shades, fashion plates in banana-yellow shorts replace the silken ao dai girls of Hue. Traveling south in Vietnam, one is effectively going West.

By the time you get to the beach resort of Nha Trang, or the hill station of Dalat, you begin to see more and more chic tourists, in Giordano T-shirts and "U.S. Mondial 94" (!) sandals, oozing wealth and modernity, as incongruous as Manhattan fashion models in a North Dakota village. They are, in fact, from Ho Chi Minh City, affluent sightseers in their own country, so different from the world around them that they seem, quite literally, to belong to a "new species" (as the Japanese call their yuppies). Around them, as the road goes south, you also begin to feel corruption in the air: Vietnamese Bruce Springsteen sound-alikes growl from every café, pirated cassettes fill the marketplace, and the line between tourist and native blurs. One is back, one senses, in Marlboro Country.

Dalat, built by the French as a summer resort in the hills— a kind of Simla East—is still a favorite holiday place for the wealthy of Saigon, who gather for photographs along the rolling lawns of the Palace Hotel, a musty, antique shooting lodge, with oil lamps and black rotary phones beside every bed, and "Bleu, bleu, l'amour est bleu . . ." always playing on the sound system. The whole city, with its tidy Provençal cottages tucked among alpine lakes and waterfalls and forests, bears almost no signs of its Eastern origins, and on a late afternoon I saw men in suits with rolled-up brollies, and women in silk gowns, assembling in the piney hillside light, outside the Catholic church, for a stylish society wedding.

For me, the most interesting tourist sight in Dalat was just that: the sight of the tourists from Saigon, making the circuit of the scenic spots—the honeymoon couples posing for photo-

graphs on tiny ponies or going for rides on romantic pad-
dleboats; the wealthy holidaymakers admiring the hibiscus and
bellflowers in the pretty gardens or posing for snapshots with
locals who impersonate themselves in cowboy hats and buckskin
jackets. Sightseers make themselves at home now—true revolutionary gesture!—in the house that once belonged to the last
emperor, Bao Dai, lounging at his desk, testing themselves
at his exercise machine, browsing through his copies of *Mrs.
Dalloway* and *La Vie de Walt Whitman*. At night, across "Sigh-
ing Lake," long-hair bands from Saigon play note-perfect versions of "Hotel California," while the racy young in drop-dead
fashions follow glamorous hostesses into darkened nightclubs.

Five hours south, the stench of kerosene, mingled with the
scent of French perfume, tells you you're in Saigon: suddenly,
the bicycles have been replaced, entirely, by scooters, and the
scooters are being steered by girls in elbow-length white gloves,
their friends hanging on to their backs as if on to excitement
itself. The bikers rev up, the lights change, the signs flash past,
and one is back, ineluctably, in Everymetropolis, Southeast
Asia—a version of Bangkok, crowded into ten tiny blocks and
hopped up to the max.

As we arrived at my hotel in the "Paris of the Orient," a
bellhop in a blue-and-golden uniform came up to open the car
door, the electronic doors of the hotel slid open, and the girl at
the reception desk, punching the keys of her computer, handed
me a coded card. There was a basket of fruit awaiting me in my
brand-new room, a wicker basket for laundry, and bottles of
toiletries in the bathroom. Luckily, however, Vietnam Tourism
has still not quite memorized its lines. I pressed the tap and
there was no hot water. I put on the TV and got nothing but
static. I looked for shampoo and found I had two bottles of
bath foam instead. And though the floor guards jumped up and
bowed each time I walked past, they could not—or would not—

read Do Not Disturb signs. Nonetheless, the hotel seemed a perfect microcosm of the new Saigon: one morning, as I walked through the lobby, it was a cacophony of saws and blowtorches and sweating laborers; by the time I returned that night, a spanking-new bar stood in one corner of the lobby, complete with tables and spacious shelves and smiling girls waiting to serve up coconut cocktails.

My first night in Saigon, a haggard man with shriveled cheeks and a baseball cap came up to me in the street. "I was in a concentration camp for eleven years," he said in perfect English. "While I was there, my wife and three children tried to escape by boat. That was the last I heard of them. I am very eager to go to your country; but I have been waiting two years, three years. The list is very long." What could I say? "How old do you think I am?" Aim low, I always tell myself. "Sixty?" He looked put out. "I am fifty-four. Maybe it was the camp that made me look so old."

There are a thousand more like him now, beached in the new order and able to find work only as *cyclo* drivers or as street peddlers of some kind. They race up to any foreigner they see, glad to have a voice at last, but when they talk, their stories sound almost like language tapes. "Let me introduce you to my niece," the old man called out after me, as I tried to make my polite escape. "She is twenty-one, a student. She would like to speak English with you."

Such legacies of the war are everywhere in Saigon: Vietnam Tourism even offers organized tours to see war orphans and a drug addicts' rehabilitation center. And the War Crimes Museum, once the U.S. Information Service, contains not only the statutory U.S. howitzers and tanks in the garden, but also six well-planned rooms methodically chronicling American atrocities: pictures of GIs carrying severed heads, detailed descriptions of American torture methods, even some Lomotil tablets belonging to "reactionary elements" and an Ozzy Osbourne T-shirt in a special case devoted to "Cultural Ideological Sabotage." But for all the *pro forma* references to "quislings" and "barbarians" and "diabolic imperialism," one feels that the bulk of the country's resentment, such as it is, is reserved for its centuries-old enemy, the Chinese; one of the most violent of the rooms in the museum is given over to Chinese atrocities and to a list of "6 Ways of Barbarous Killings Used by the Chinese Aggressors."

Besides, the main ideology apparent in Saigon is sheer survivalism. On May Day, the only parade that I could find in town was the reckless procession of motorbikes. And on Liberation Day, the sixteenth anniversary of the moment when North Vietnamese tanks dramatically crashed through the gates of the Presidential Palace and retook the south, I went to the Museum of the Revolution, the War Crimes Museum, and the Reunification Hall itself in search of some celebration. But there was not a single thing in sight. Just another quiet day as usual, busloads of villagers from the countryside filing through what was once President Thieu's private cinema to watch a stirring twenty-minute video about the Revolution (featuring priceless footage of French garden parties and "Nich-xon," looking shifty forty years ago). Was there no commemoration of the day? Not in secular Saigon. "It was a sad day for me," said a woman who pointed out the 555 cigarettes in which the Vietcong had disseminated details of their plans. "Before 1975 I was a teacher. Now I am just a museum guide. We have nothing to celebrate."

Ho Chi Minh City, in fact, is a shameless refutation of everything that Ho Chi Minh stood and fought for. Yet it bears out what nearly everyone who fought here concluded: that the driving, ruling passion in Vietnam is not for any imported political system but simply for Vietnam. Nationalism, not Marxism, is what drove people to lay down their lives, and almost every

Vietnamese might bear the *nom de guerre* that Ho Chi Minh took for himself, Nguyen Ai Quoc (Nguyen the Patriot). If Marxism has to be scrapped in pursuit of nationalism, so be it. "We build socialism in a flexible way," a Vietnamese friend told me when I asked him how he could reconcile the explosion of free enterprise with the country's notional Communism. "If we were to have socialism as in the Soviet Union, our country would collapse." Nothing if not pragmatic, I thought. "If you are rich," he continued smoothly, "you will make the country rich."

And though the inflation rate may be 200 percent, a former Vietcong official told me, "there is no social disturbance here. People in Europe cannot understand it. But the reason is the parallel economy." The black market, fueled by remittances from Vietnamese abroad, allows people to live, very often, like kings almost, in five-story villas, with cars of their own, their savings kept in dollars, sapphires, and gold. And everything is negotiable in Vietnam. When I asked a Hanoi guide for a receipt, he instantly said, "You need I write more or you need I write less?" When I told him that the actual figure would do nicely, he looked decidedly disappointed.

Thus the only word for Saigon is "wild." One evening I counted more than a hundred two-wheel vehicles racing past me in the space of sixty seconds, speeding round the jam-packed streets as if on some crazy merry-go-round, a mad carnival without a ringmaster; I walked into a dance club and found myself in the midst of a crowded floor of hip gay boys in sleeveless T-shirts doing the latest moves to David Byrne; outside again, I was back inside the generic Asian swirl, walking through tunnels of whispers and hisses. "You want boom-boom?" "Souvenir for your dah-ling?" "Why you not take special massage?" Shortly before midnight, the taxi girls stream out of their nightclubs in their party dresses and park their scooters outside the hotels along "Simultaneous Uprising" Street. Inside, Indian and

Malaysian and Japanese trade-fair delegates huddle in clusters, circling like excited schoolboys and checking out the mini-skirted wares, while out on the street legless beggars hop about, and crippled girls offer oral services, and boys of every stripe mutter bargains for their sisters. One wanders, dazed, as through some crazed Fellini night-world, beautiful women in golden ao dais waving slowly from slow-moving *cyclos*.

The bottom line of all this commotion is, of course, hard currency, and it is business that makes the whole whirligig go round. Saigon's streets teem with stalls selling everything from Chinese goldfish and tubes of Volgate toothpaste to "Country Music" tapes and mysterious beans, so many anarchic goods that they spill off the sidewalks and block all traffic. But the most common items to be found are books entitled *Making Investments in Ho Chi Minh Ville* and *Export Import 1991 Directory*. Near the antique shops there are Microcomputer and Software Service Centers; inside the department stores, next to a hundred styles of sandals, are English-language manuals and books on *How to Survive in the U.S.A.*, knocking against tomes like *A Guide to Investment Co-operation* and *An Investor's Guide to Vietnam*. "In Saigon, if you have money, you can do anything," said a Vietnamese friend of mine from Da Nang, a little wistfully.

It is that kind of heedless consumerism that is redecorating the city daily, and Saigon, like more and more of the south, seems to be learning—or relearning—how to make itself pleasant and available to foreigners (as neighboring Thailand has done so artfully): the bookshops are full now of soft-focus old French books on l'Indochine, the stalls sell this week's editions of *Time* and *Newsweek*, the people adapt themselves with a courtesan's suppleness to one's needs. It is common to hear that Saigon is returning to the hoary vitality of the war; but it might be more accurate to say that none of that ever left, and now it is just coming out again ("coming out" like a debutante, like a sexual renegade, like an old habit effaced by something foreign). A city that has had intimate relations with the West for so long cannot easily remain innocent of complications; and much of Saigon has the feel of a palimpsest—what was once the elegant French Rue Catinat, and during the war was the freewheeling Tu Do or "Freedom" Street, is now Dong Khoi or "Simultaneous Uprising" Street.

Yet for all the nonstop hustle-bustle, and for all the crooked smiles that can make Saigon seem like a giant cathedral of the profane, the town is, like Bangkok a few years ago, ultimately irresistible—it simply overwhelms you with the persistence of its energy. You can no more rebuff it than you can a runaway train on a downhill slope. It's hard, it's made up, it's cunning, you tell yourself, and then you go out into the streets and find yourself swept up in the sheer power and vigor of it all. On Sunday nights at six o'clock, all the motorbikes careen toward Notre Dame Cathedral in what was once John F. Kennedy Square, and there, in a novel version of the drive-in church, the parishioners simply park their bikes outside the church's doors and stand in rows, beside their wheels, a hundred or more of them lined up in the street, the sermon broadcast through huge speakers almost entirely drowned out by the roar of traffic all around. Little kids skip around on holiday nights, blowing soap bubbles, making paper caterpillars, or posing, coquettish, in tiny, flouncy dresses. And often I found myself just standing on the street for twenty minutes or more, all but transfixed by the whole motorized carousel whizzing past. One of the most dangerous adventures in Vietnam is simply trying to cross the street in Saigon.

And for all the constant changes, Saigon is still gracious with the pleasures of an acacia-lined French town. There are the *patisseries* offering delicious *baguettes* and strong French coffee; there are the neon-lit boats, scarlet and white, that cruise along the Saigon River after dark, scattering a magic swirl of colors. In the early afternoon, a siesta sleepiness falls over the place, as the beauty-parlor girls recline on their chairs. And at night, you can go for drinks at the rooftop bar of the Rex Hotel, once a U.S. bachelor officers' quarters and still a decidedly zany place, with Saigon beauties smiling at every available male, and statues of nude figures and prancing elephants around the bonsai trees. On hot afternoons, I often stopped off in a garden café and sipped *citrons pressés* to the sound of "Me and You and a Dog Named Boo" or some husky latter-day Piaf, as the day's heat began to lift and the local sparks to show off their latest acquisitions.

Saigon is still a highly raffish sailors' port of characters and stories, many of them unchanged since the war. There is the man who runs the pancake restaurant in a shed that doubles as a bus depot for a touring rock band, where tables are placed next to two shiny buses, with beauty tips from Miss Vietnam along the wall. There is the all-knowing, wily Mr. Fix-it, who has wild turkeys strutting around his floor and sells crocodile-skin briefcases, thousand-dollar tigers (complete with heads), caviar, motorbikes, and almost anything licit and illicit (he gave me the latest dirt on some colleagues in New York). There is the man who trades in endangered species (ocelots, gibbons, and crocodiles), and the veteran *mama-san* who runs the same girlie bar that she ran during the war (frequented often by the same men, returning GIs looking to relive old times). And there is the famous Madame Dai, once a leading Opposition parliamentarian, who now offers tourists dinner in her home, amidst a mess of eccentric bric-a-brac—masks, pots, joss sticks, and books in French on maritime law—and chatters away in French to customers who take ten minutes to order, inviting them upstairs for informal concerts afterwards.

The Saigon shops are madcap, and every time you go into one, you never know what you'll find inside: ancient Brownie Hawkeye cameras, and 315 ml. cans of Coke in front of Mona Lisa string curtains; unsolicited companions who saunter along as, down the street, you hear the opening strains of "If you're going to San Francisco, be sure to wear some flowers in your hair." In a bookshop, a bare-chested, wild-haired owner motions to an assistant to beam a flashlight along the shelves so that you can read titles like *Japan Unmasked;* in the thirty-two-kiosk Central Post Office (with one booth for "Paging Services," one for "Formalities for Payment of Money Orders," one for "Subscriptions to Newspapers and Reviews"), as you exit, made-up girls on scooters give you long, inquiring gazes. Cinemas have living subtitles, men (or tapes of men) who deliver all the dialogue, and there is a mosque in central Saigon, and a pagoda full of joss-stick baskets. In Saigon, in a single day, I met an Italian entrepreneur who'd gone into Kuwait just six hours before Saddam Hussein's men arrived (and, having finally been released, promptly took off for this other war zone); the now famous former *Time* correspondent who, on the day of the U.S. departure, revealed that he'd been a Vietcong colonel all along (he still drives his '55 Peugeot, talks about piastres, and asks after his long-lost friends); and the Beverly Hills resident who'd been busted for sending dope out in airmail envelopes his first week in Kathmandu.

"It's kind of spooky sometimes," a Canadian lawyer said to me one day. "There you are, in the Kim Do Hotel, it's ninety-three degrees outside, and it's April eighth, and you're listening to a Vietnamese cover version of 'Jingle Bells.' "

Perhaps the best symbol of today's Five O'Clock Follies in Saigon is Maxim's, not so much a restaurant as a four-ring Vietnamese Vegas, with 242 dishes on its menu and a flurry of twelve-piece orchestras racing on and off its stage. The first

time I went there, an elegantly ao daied girl led me to a table
in a room full of banqueting families. I perused the enormous
menu—Braised Pig Legs with Black Moss, Steamed Silky Fowl
with Herb Soup, Tendon of Deer with Sea Sleegs (or Fish
Tripe), Pig Brain with Crab Meat Soup. Every few minutes,
one of the thirty or so waitresses, decked out this night in pink
chiffon, came over and dropped a hot towel in my lap, or poured
some more of my Coke into my Air France glass. Someone else
brought a plate of cashews, a plate of celery, a plate of something
orange. Onstage, an eight-piece orchestra was banging out some
plaintive melody, led by a girl playing a xylophone. A tall old
man, with glasses and slicked-back hair and the weariness of
someone who has been playing Bogart since 1949, came over
to take my order. The orchestra went off and was replaced by
an eleven-piece band and a series of new chanteuses, vamping
it up and gyrating to old favorites like "Let's Twist Again," while
backed by projected slides of Singapore. It was a little like
watching some Oriental version of Ed McMahon's *Star Search*,
performed only by applicants for the Hong Kong Playboy Club,
following one another in a furious, unrelenting procession, belting out show-stopping versions of "Yesterday Once More," then
racing off to play at the next club down. Yesterday once more
indeed: the former GIs at the next table were engaged in a
heated debate about the merits of Mama Cass.

All this, of course, will change as quickly as you can say
"Investment," and Ho Chi Minh City, more than anywhere, is
a butterfly waiting to emerge from its chrysalis. As it is, the city
already feels plugged into the international circuit, and not just
in its IDD phones and IATA schedules. Already, you can stay
at the ultramodern Floating Hotel, shipped over here from the
Great Barrier Reef, with cable TV, Filipina deejays, and "Pizza
by the Pool" lunches that cost as much as a month's supply of
meals on the street. And already there are Melrose-flashy cafés

offering Angel Hair Pasta and Tex-Mex Omelets and Medallions of Beef with Green Peppercorns. It is impossible not to feel that Saigon, with its Ca-Li-Pho-Nia Ham-Bu-Go stores and its karaoke bars, its Chiclets kids and waterski clubs, its privately owned Mercedeses and hustlers in "Atlanta Placons" baseball caps—Saigon, with its rogue economy—is the image of the country's future.

Saigon is also beginning to become a foreigners' hangout of sorts. House for Rent signs are beginning to appear, and English-teaching gigs; many resourceful Americans are finding a way to spend weeks, or even months, at a time just hanging out here. And there is a world of variety in the vicinity. Along the Mekong Delta, you can see islands lush with plums, durians, mangoes, and papayas, and visit a "typical farmer's home," complete with Snoopy pillows and postcards of Berlin. All along the island, bursting out with jackfruit, pineapple, and black pepper trees, roofs are made of coconut leaves, bridges of coconut trunks, even tea cozies out of coconuts. To the south is the beach resort the French called Cap St. Jacques, well on its way to becoming the new Pattaya. And to the northwest, in Tay Ninh, you can visit perhaps the single most colorful and extraordinary sight in all Vietnam, the rococo, Disney-worthy holy see of the Cao Dai faith, a "Third Alliance between God and Man" whose deities include Lao-tzu, Jesus, Sun Yat-sen, Joan of Arc, Shakespeare, and—head of them all—Victor Hugo, who transmit their wisdom to white-robed priests in séances. The faith once had a following of up to two million, commanded a private army, and all but ruled the province of Tay Ninh. On the way to this unlikely Vatican, you can see the Cu Chi tunnels, part of a two-hundred-mile network of underground rooms, furnished—incredibly—with whole kitchens, rest rooms, conference rooms, and theaters. Foreigners are encouraged to crawl through a specially enlarged fifty-yard stretch of tunnels, which leaves most of them half dead with claustrophobia; the Vietnamese guerrillas lived in them for weeks. Against such unearthly determination, one begins to feel, there can be no defense. And anyone who wonders where that resourcefulness has gone today need only look at the lighters made of bullets, and oil lamps of rockets, that they try to flog in places like the "Cu Chi Shop and Friendship and Sentiments."

In the end, though, much of Saigon feels almost like a Vietnamese community in California (from which, after all, many of its funds still come). And it was hard for me to think of Saigon as part of Vietnam. In Vietnam, people stare at you because they have seldom seen a foreigner before; in Saigon, they stare because they know exactly what a foreigner is worth. In Vietnam, everything is shut by 10:00 p.m.; in Saigon, the fun is just beginning then ("it's a city of pleasure that reaches its peak at night," wrote Marguerite Duras). In Vietnam, you can hardly hear English spoken; in Saigon, English classes are all the rage. In Vietnam, indeed, you cannot spend money if you want to; in Saigon, you cannot save it. Ultimately, the main difference, for me, was that in Vietnam you do not feel you have to pay for smiles.

The seductions of Saigon are so loud and brazen that they tend to efface the shyer effects of the countryside; after a few days in the hurly-burly rush, I could scarcely remember what Vietnam was like. I went to Vietnam, though, to get away from noise, from sophistication, and from the state-of-the-art frenzy of much of modern Asia. And the very raciness and flash that make Saigon so exciting to many Vietnamese—the Ghosts of Bangkok Past and Future—make me, when returning to the country in my mind, take shelter instead amidst the quiet pride and unforced hospitality of Hanoi and of Hue.

UP FOR SALE, OR ADOPTIO

> "Yes, it's very peaceful," my
> Aunt said, "only an occasional
> gun-shot after dark."
>
> GRAHAM GREENE

I was staying in the Gran Hotel del Paraguay. It wasn't grand, it wasn't really a hotel, but it was certainly Paraguayan. Four dogs were sprawled out in the comfort of the lobby. A few gray-haired women from Germany were poring over a small library that offered copies of *San Juan Shootout* and *Reagan's Reign of Error*. A fan was turning, very slowly, above us all. "We are certainly going to be the worthy hosts our clientele expects," said the signs in every room. "Without improvising. And much more."

The Gran Hotel was renowned as the former residence of Madame Eliza Lynch, *La Concubina Irlandesa*, an Irish courtesan brought back from the Boulevard Saint-Germain by the nineteenth-century president Francisco Solano López. He was the fat young man with bad teeth whose qualities, as listed by R. B. Cunninghame-Graham, included "sadism, an inverted patriotism, colossal ignorance of the outside world, a megalomania pushed almost to insanity, a total disregard of human life or human dignity [and] an abject cowardice that in any other country in the world but Paraguay would have rendered him ridiculous." His great achievement, so far as I could see, was meddling in Uruguay's civil war and so involving Paraguay in a war in which it fought against not one, not two, but three of its neighbors—Brazil, Argentina, and Uruguay itself—and at whose end its population of 800,000 had been reduced to one of 194,000, of which exactly 2,100 were adult men. As a result of this, in the words of the *South American Handbook*, López was "the most venerated of Paraguay's heroes."

Madame Lynch was, accordingly, a kind of *ex officio* heroine, a goddess by association. She had helped her lover in his cause by importing two fellow trollops from Paris to start a "finishing school" and by executing many of the Asunción society ladies who felt that an Irish strumpet was not the ideal partner for the "Napoleon of the Americas."

Strolling out of the palatial grounds of her mansion, I made my way into the heart of the capital. The place was like nothing I had ever seen before. It was not just that none of the traffic lights was working, or even that straw-haired Mennonites in sky-blue-and-white clothes—like apparitions from some seventeenth-century Dutch landscape painting—were sauntering hand-in-hand across the street. It was not even the fact that every store that was not called "Alemán" seemed to have its sign in Korean hangul script. It was simply that Paraguay seemed indifferent—or impervious, at least—to life as it is lived around the planet.

The famous sign that for many years showed President Stroessner's face next to the slogan PEACE . . . WORK . . . WELL-BEING had been taken down from the center of the city, the Plaza of the Heroes, when Stroessner fled the country in 1989. But the Stroessner legacy lived on. The showcase cinema in the plaza, the Cine Victoria, was showing *S.O.S. Sexual Emergency*, *Tension and Desire*, and *Bedtime Tales* (with doubleheaders around the clock on Fridays and Saturdays) and had lurid posters of its previous hard-core offerings gazing out upon the public. Shoe-shine boys in T-shirts that said, enigmatically, CAT'S FACE LIFT were sprawled around a statue consecrated to the Twelfth Congress of the World Anti-Communist League. In one corner of the Plaza of the Heroes, a man was selling bank notes from around the world and a picture of Winston Churchill. In another stood a Seiko clock commemorating the fifteenth anniversary of the Brotherhood Pact between Asunción and the town of Chiba, in Japan.

The dominant feature of the Plaza of the Heroes, however, was a huge monument, modeled on Les Invalides in Paris, known as the Pantheon of the Heroes. Inside its sepulchral entrance, past two ramrod soldiers in full uniform, I came upon memorials to all the country's great men: Dr. Francia, the country's first president, who had quickly had himself named Dictator for Life and had every dog in the country executed. His successor, Carlos López, described by an English scientist as "immensely fat" and another dictator who had ruled without ministers or advisers. His son and heir, Francisco, regarded by his faithful British retainer, George Thompson, as a "monster without parallel." And General José Félix Estigarribia, who led Paraguay to a triumphant nonvictory in the Chaco War.

Around the Pantheon there were plaques, more plaques than I had seen in any one place since the Tower of the Juche Idea in Pyongyang. Their donors read like a roll call of the founding members of the World Anti-Communist League: there were plaques from the Taiwanese chief of staff, from *peronistas* in Argentina, from right-wing groups in Israel; plaques congratulating López junior on his sixtieth birthday (though he died at forty-two), plaques congratulating him on his 146th anniversary, plaques congratulating him on every one of his heroic deeds (such as executing hundreds of his own people, including his two brothers).

Outside the Pantheon there stretched block after block after clamorous block of money changers' stores, gold dealers, and shops peddling smuggled goods, pirated perfumes, war memorabilia, and pumas. The streets outside the shops overflowed with stalls selling counterfeit tapes, musical condoms, and copies of *Playboy* from around the world. A few Indians were selling bows and arrows near a bust commemorating another hero, Juan E. O'Leary. Men were circling around, muttering, somewhat hopelessly, *"Cambio, cambio."* Every shop in Our Lady of the Assumption, as I'd surmised from Iguazú, seemed to be called Casa—Casa Mo., Casa Solomon, Casa Fanny; Casa Kuo Ping, Casa Porky, Casa Hung Ching. Imagine a used-car lot in a border town, and you are well on your way to imagining the center of the Paraguayan capital.

The most conspicuous stores, though, were the money changers' outlets. Money changing is one of the great traditional art forms of Paraguay, and almost a folkloric spectacle. I decided to enjoy this native skill in a place called Cambios Guarani. This seemed a good choice because everything in Paraguay was apparently called Guarani—the local language, the currency, the main hotel, even the soda water. It also seemed apt because Cambios Guarani was said to be owned by the country's president.

Inside, things were marginally less busy than on the floor of the New York Stock Exchange. Eighteen customers were storming the front desk, where men in ties were counting out stacks of money slightly larger than the GNP of Peru. Around the store, men with briefcases were loitering in the corners. A German woman was asking, somewhat desperately, for Hans. The signs outlining the rules for transactions were printed in six languages.

I signed two American Express traveler's checks and gave them over to a smart young teller. He asked for my passport and my bill of receipt for the purchase of the checks. He then went off and returned with photocopies of my passport and of my bill of receipt. Then he handed me a slip, which I took to another man in order to receive my two hundred dollars in guarani.

A little way off the Plaza of the Heroes, just past the Internal Tax Office (a perfect replica of La Scala in Milan), was the main cathedral in Asunción: Paraguay is one country where the cathedral does not enjoy pride of place (it is also a country where, in the yellow pages, banks take up five times more space than churches; in my relatively secular California hometown, by comparison, the list of churches is three times longer than that of banks). The cathedral was a strangely disheveled place, emptier and more neglected even than its counterpart in Communist Havana. The signs describing Jesus' passion were all in French.

Outside, in the Plaza Independencia, a young man was urinating against the Legislative Palace, and cooing lovers were sitting on green benches, taking in the romantic view of a squatters' slum of shacks held together by pieces of cardboard that said PHILIPS.

Across the plaza was the most famous museum in Paraguay, the Museum of Military History. Its first room was devoted to Dr. Francia ("El Supremo" to his friends), who, in the careful words of the sign, "governed implacably against the enemies of the new country." Most of the rest of the Museum of Military History was given over to paintings and relics of *La Concubina Irlandesa:* her toilet was here, and her dishes, her fan, her comb, her shawl, her jug. Her music box was also here, and an album signed by 87,000 Paraguayans in homage to her (which, given the population at the end of the War of the Triple Alliance and the percentage that could write, was certainly an impressive figure). In another room were Francisco Solano López pajamas.

Behind the Museum of Military History, along the Río Paraguay, was the Government Palace (a homage to the Louvre, which, due to the chaos of the War of the Triple Alliance, had

taken sixty years to build and had to be constructed, in part, by
boys of six). Half a block away was a store selling coats made
entirely of endangered species—jaguars, ocelots, and the like—
bright with rhinestone buttons. Around the shady parks, the
local citizenry was deep in such local publications as *Crónica*,
a weekly paper that consists of almost nothing but pictures of
bodies, ravaged (if male) and about to be (if female). Through
the swarming, narrow streets cruised cool blondes in Mercedeses, not always observing the speed limit (which was 6 ¼
miles per hour).

At night, the streets of Asunción were hopping—quite literally: two little girls dressed from head to foot in a Philips cardboard box were jumping down the block. A woman was picking
lice out of her daughter's hair. Young boys were cadging lifts
on the backs of garbage trucks. Here and there, night-school
typists were tapping away at twenty or thirty words an hour.

Occasionally, the traffic lights even came to life.

Deciding to pass up the Bolero Chinese Restaurant, I went
instead to the Kung Fu. At the entrance, an expressionless
Chinese couple ushered me into the main banquet hall, and a
friendly Syrian boy who could not speak Arabic led me to a
table with a rose. The Syrian boy removed the rose, the Chinese
couple closed the door so they could sing along with the Muzak,
and I found myself alone in an elaborate chamber of red lanterns
and mock T'ang dynasty paintings. From the kitchen, a dog
barked plaintively.

After deciding that I would avoid "Wong Ton Fritos," I asked
my hosts where the bathroom was. They ushered me into a
room that was indeed perfect for a bath: it included a large tub,
an electric shower, and a bidet.

Walking back to the Gran Hotel, I strolled along Avenida
Mariscal López, the grandest street in Paraguay. It would be
the grandest street in almost any country, with its block-long

houses, its boomtown malls, its ghostly mansions hidden behind iron gates. Like the main highway in Paraguay—in fact, like almost everything in Paraguay—it is named after Francisco Solano López, who decided to award himself the title of Marshal. One intersection was dominated by a statue of the country's great hero atop his charging steed.

Back in the Gran Hotel, the receptionist greeted me in Hindi, a cockroach was waiting to welcome me in my bedroom, and a sudden thunderstorm turned the hotel corridors into rivers, a few dead leaves floating past my door. In the beautiful dining room, where La Madama had once held masked balls and taught *le tout Asunción* to polka, four men in ponchos were putting on a show of Paraguayan culture, featuring songs from Mexico, songs from Cuba, and songs from Peru. One of them made deafening bird noises which echoed round and around the painted ceilings and linoleum floors. Much of the music was drowned out, however, by the squawks of babies.

For the Gran Hotel del Paraguay was crawling, quite literally, with the things: there were more babies here than you'd find in a maternity ward—babies seated in strollers at every table, babies in the garden, and babies in the lobby, dark-skinned babies most of them, being clucked over by excited couples from England, Germany, and most often, America. It seemed a fit tribute to *La Concubina Irlandesa* (though when his first son was born, Francisco Solano López had ordered a 101-gun salute, and eleven buildings were destroyed). On every side, I heard talk of paperwork, trips to the embassy, court cases. The babies screamed, the parents cooed. Finally, I got it: this pleasant residential hotel, with its lavish gardens, its playground, and its unreasonably reasonable rates, was the center for a lucrative adoption trade. In Paraguay, where everything could be had for a price, the latest boom market was in babies.

I suppose I had always been drawn to Paraguay. It is one of the forgotten corners of the world, one of the unplumbed shadows, one of "the et ceteras in the list of nations," as Isabel Hilton quotes someone calling it. No one seems to know exactly where the landlocked, time-bound hideout is, though those in the know will tell you that Uruguay is the good angel of Latin America, and Paraguay, the dark; that one is a resort, and the other a refuge. Certainly Paraguay is in some sense a country off the map. When I asked my travel agent about flights to Asunción, she told me I could either go by LAP (the airline founded by Stroessner) or by Ladeco (which seemed to translate as "Kitchen Utensils Airways"). When I went to my local bookstore to look for volumes on the place, I found four books on Peru, four on Belize, forty-five on Mexico, one book on the Galápagos Islands, and not a single one on Paraguay.

During the thirty-five-year reign of Alfredo Stroessner, in which, every sixty days, the president had dutifully renewed a state of siege, Paraguay had all but seceded from the world and turned into a kind of bad playwright's version of a sleepy, crooked military despotism, a Central Casting vision of chicanery. When Paul Mazursky wanted to make a spoof of Latin American corruption, he called his movie *Moon Over Parador*, peopled it with figures called Strausmann, Dieter Lopez, and Madam Loop, and portrayed Paraguay as a kind of Shangri-la in reverse, an invert's paradise ("One day in New York is like a year in Parador," says Richard Dreyfuss). The only trouble was, reality put Hollywood to shame. As fast as the other Latin countries moved toward democracy in the eighties, Paraguay slipped ever deeper into torpor and a criminal dictatorship. In 1989, Stroessner, the longest-ruling tyrant in the world, except for Kim Il Sung (whom he was coming to resemble—the one so far to the right and the other so far to the left that they almost seemed to meet), was visiting his favorite mistress for his usual Thursday afternoon siesta when he heard that he had been ousted by his protégé, and the father-in-law of his son, General Andres Rodríguez. During the coup, the elite corps' tanks were unable to move because the man who had the keys to them was out of town. After the coup, the red-tied Colorado Party faithful who had previously danced the Don Alfredo Polka quickly changed their steps to do the Rodríguez Polka (with lyrics that ran: "May God help you and also the Armed Forces!").

Paraguay, in fact, mocked soap opera's gaudiest inventions. But there was more to its mystique than simple heavy-handedness: Paraguay had the reputation of being the darkest country on the planet. Colombia, of course, was a contender, with its blue-black clouds hanging over Bogotá, its international conferences on witchcraft, its schools for pickpockets, and its second city boasting the highest murder rate in the world. But Colombia also had ruins and beaches and museums, a patina of civilization. Nigeria and Indonesia were said to be the world leaders in corruption; but they at least were huge nations with lots of oil. Paraguay, by comparison, was a kind of minor-league, farm-team, up-and-coming criminal—"like Madame Tussaud's," as one friend said, "except all the figures are living." This was the place where deposed dictators found a new home (Somoza from Nicaragua, Perón from Argentina). This was the place where fugitive Nazis received a hearty welcome—Eduard Roschmann, "the Butcher of Riga," allegedly died here; Josef Mengele, "the Angel of Death," was a Paraguayan citizen for much of the time he was the world's most wanted war criminal; and Martin Bormann lived just across the border. This was also the place where Italian neo-Fascists gave lectures, Croatian thugs trained security details, Chinese tong kings picked up tips, and the new president himself—the "clean" one—was associated with drug kingpins who'd made $145 million in shipments of heroin. When Nietzsche's sister wanted to set up an Aryan colony with her husband, "the professional anti-Semite" Bernhard Förster (I read in Ben Macintyre's engaging book, *Forgotten Fatherland*), where did they come—where could they come—but Paraguay?

In California, I knew of a Retirement Home for Performing Animals; Paraguay sounded like a Retirement Home for Performing Criminals.

My first taste of the mutant state, across from Iguazú Falls, had not been disappointing. Throughout our visit, my driver, a friendly family man from Argentina, had darkened the afternoon with tales of Paraguayan lawlessness. "Can't the police do anything to stop the crime?" I asked. He laughed bitterly. "The police are the ones who are performing the crime!" Throughout the trip, too, he refused to leave the car, on the safe assumption that it would almost certainly be stolen. He visited Paraguay almost every day, and his wife was Paraguayan, but he was not about to take any chances. "And this is daytime," he said as I took in the unholy chaos. "At night, it is not even safe to leave your room."

Perhaps the ultimate depiction of the land of corpses laureled in orange petals, however, had come from Graham Greene. For Greene, the moral ironist, Paraguay was the end of the line, spiritually speaking, the place where all roads terminate. In *Travels with My Aunt*, he delivers the definitive portrait of a land where crooks wear pictures of the General, and a Czech is hoping to import two million plastic straws. "The only old beautiful building . . . proved, as I came closer to it, to be the prison," says Greene's mild-mannered narrator, Henry Pulling. Later, we learn that "They don't have coroners in Paraguay" and that smuggling is a national industry. "In this blessed land of Paraguay," says a war criminal, "there is no income tax and no evasions are necessary." Greene could no more leave Paraguay than he could leave loneliness, or flight, or the question of evil.

Yet it was not always so. When I went to my hometown library to look up books on Paraguay, the kind of titles I found were *The Lost Paradise, A Vanished Arcadia, Picturesque Paraguay.* For decades, even centuries, Paraguay—like any country, perhaps, where people can derive something out of nothing—had been regarded as a utopia just waiting to be realized, an empty space waiting to be converted into a private paradise. "When I first came to Asunción from Spain," wrote the Paraguayan poet Josefina Plá, "I realized that I'd arrived in Paradise. The air was warm, the light was tropical, and the shuttered, colonial houses suggested sensual, tranquil lives." Even G. K. Chesterton, who never saw the place, more or less rehearsed the conventional wisdom when he wrote: "Ye bade the Red Man rise like the Red Clay . . . And man lost Paradise in Paraguay."

The whole of eastern Paraguay, among the best-watered areas in the world, resembled a luxuriant tropical Eden; the west lacked even running water. In both areas, however, Paraguay seemed a place of absolutes. Voltaire was fascinated by this notional Arcadia, which he described as both Elysium and its opposite; Thomas Carlyle wrote an entire book on Dr. Francia, who ruled over his homemade land with a kind of mythic force (decreeing that no one could look at him in the street). That Paraguay was a byword for the Possible—more Paradise than Parador—was best suggested by the fact that Robert Southey, the British poet laureate at the time, called his longest poem *A Tale of Paraguay* ("For in history's mournful map, the eye / On Paraguay, as on a sunny spot, / May rest complacent").

In fact, in history's mournful eye, Paraguay was perhaps the most sunless place on earth, its history a sad tale of what men will do with the prospect of paradise and what follies they visit upon a virgin land. The story of Paraguay is the story of the vanity of human wishes, one utopian chimera following another. First came the Spaniards, who promptly availed themselves of the friendliness of the local Indians, setting up harems in which each *conquistador* kept twenty native wives, or more (the "Father of the Nation," Governor Irala, earned the title in part by fathering at least eight *mestizos*). Then came the Jesuits, who organized the artistically minded Guarani into *reducciones*, or crafts-based communes, which crumbled as soon as the Jesuits left. Then came the strongmen who, like Dr. Francia, scribbled their initials all over the open country. And finally there followed the steady stream of refugees from Germany or Australia or Italy who sought to build a new Arcadia here and founded their own custom-made utopias in Nueva Germania, Nueva Australia, Nueva Italia.

In almost every case, the dream went sour. Dr. Francia began by sealing off all the country's borders, expelling all foreigners and committing the country to solitary confinement. Carlos López, who came next, was described as "more utterly alone than any man in the world." His son, Francisco, ended up fleeing through the countryside, to the town still known as Isla Madama, taking along his mother and his sisters in wooden cages. By the end of the War of the Triple Alliance, Paraguay had lost the Iguazú Falls, and its national anthem was written by a Uruguayan.

In 1932, just as the wounds from the Triple Alliance were beginning to heal, Paraguay promptly got involved in another war, with Bolivia, over a piece of land that neither of them wanted. Some 85,000 men were killed, and Paraguay found itself on the bleeding end of two of the three major wars fought on the continent (while the Chaco, over which the battle had raged, was revealed to be an entirely desolate and inhospitable scrubland without resources of any kind). A little later, the country entered a civil war, in which roughly a fifth of its people fled into Argentina. Meanwhile, Paraguay saw thirty-one presidents in fifty-years—seven between 1910 and 1912 alone—in a cycle of instability that ended only when Stroessner took over. Thus the melancholy pattern dragged on: the country either had no government at all or a government that saw itself in block capitals. "Dictatorship is to Paraguay what constitutional democracy is to Scandinavia or Britain," says the U.S. Library of Congress survey.

The Stroessner regime was the same old story, a tale of good intentions gone awry and of a man who started out industrious, instituted reforms, brought constancy to the economy—twenty-two years without inflation—but gradually became more and more caught up in power and isolation, until he ended up lost in a hall of golden mirrors, his country turned into a cemetery. The monomania, the public mistresses, the brutal elimination of enemies, the commissioning of books in which he was called "THE LUMINOUS LIGHTHOUSE"—no one could deny that Stroessner was faithful to Paraguayan tradition.

If Paraguay is a paradise today, it is mostly one for ironists. For it offers absurdities almost too good to be true and schools its residents in the higher forms of sarcasm. "Anything, *anything* you can get here is illegal," a delightedly "polluted" academic told me. In the central market of town, he said, almost gleefully, "No one can go in, not even the police. It's entirely lawless there. The people pay no taxes, nothing is registered, anything can happen." Argentine goods are cheaper in Paraguay than in Argentina, but Paraguayan sugar is cheaper outside Paraguay. Paraguay exports soya beans, but it has no soya crops. When paychecks are delivered, receptionists routinely loot the envelopes before they can be handed out. And when the opposition newspaper *ABC Color* was closed down by the government

In 1984, many government bigwigs came to the publisher in secret and offered to sell him paper mills on the cheap.

I didn't take the celebrated "Tour of the Houses that Corruption Built," which is the first stop of almost every foreign journalist in Paraguay. But still, I found, one cannot drive around the city without receiving a crash course in the popular folklore. This was the place where Somoza was gunned down, this was the house where the Argentine hit men lived for a year while tracking him. This was the house where Stroessner's favorite mistress lived—the daughter of his former mistress—and this was the house that Stroessner promised to his illegitimate daughter. This was Stroessner's own home (a massive park that goes on and on and on for more than two blocks, with a police station next door and, across the street, the U.S. embassy— "the largest in the world," by some accounts—waiting to polka with the dictator). The newest highlight of the circle tour is the home of General Rodríguez, just off Avenida General Genes, in a thicket of satellite dishes and generals' palaces, opposite a Chinese gangster's pagoda, and within sight of the Central Bank (a twenty-five-acre spread big enough to house a university, its massive buildings sitting like *Titanics* stranded in a vacant lot, and equipped with an Olympic-size swimming pool).

Paraguay today, therefore, has the equivocal aspect of a whole country decorated like a closing sale—All Stock Must Go! Positively Last Prices!—and governed by rules that run counter to those of the world at large. "If you brought the Queen of England to Paraguay, she would run contraband too," the secretary of the new president had memorably declared. "Paraguay is full of witches," a sorcerer had told Norman Lewis. More serious charges had been brought by human rights activists and scholars, who claimed that Paraguay was home to slavery, child brothels, and genocide as recently as the seventies. At the very least, there was a sense that this was a place where anything could be bought—passports, identities, babies. Everyone had a price in Paraguay, and usually it was radically discounted.

Thus the TAP "Guide to Paraguay" began, pointedly: "On visiting Paraguay, tourists may have several aims, in addition to recreation, resting and renewing energy." The only trouble was, there were no tourists in Paraguay. The "Land of Sun, and of Adventures," as its official slogan has it, maintains not a single tourist office around the world; the only office within the country consists of a sullen man sitting (occasionally) at a desk under a stairwell and telling you not to take more than two of the dusty brochures in front of him. "Asunción is home to hundreds of places worth visiting," the book in my hotel room hopefully suggested; unfortunately, even the ever-diligent Lonely Planet guide could find only three "things to see" in Asunción—and one of them was a double bill of bad American movies at the cinema. During all the time I spent in Paraguay, I met only one other sightseer—a fantastically merry *peronista* from Buenos Aires named Daniel Ortega, with whom I dined in the hotel where Nietzsche's brother-in-law committed suicide. ("There is a book in Buenos Aires, a best-seller," said Sr. Ortega, a student of the human comedy, "that was written by Bush's dog!" In the very next sentence he was telling me that there was a hole in Belém, in Brazil, that reached to the center of the earth—he had read this in another Argentine best-seller, by Charles Berlitz.)

Yet as I spent more time in the country, I began, very slowly, to fall into its rhythm and its spell, and to see more and more advantages to being neglected by the world. I took to relaxing in the sauna of a five-star hotel with a copy of *Business Week* only three years old, and to inching through the side streets on a Saturday night in a '72 Chevy, which gave out at every corner, all the warning lights on its dashboard flashing at once and parts

of the car rolling around beneath me while the radio throbbed,
"Gonna take you into the danger zone!" And as I started to talk
to foreign experts on the place, I began to find that Paraguay
was a kind of cult favorite among many old Latin American
hands, the hidden (costume) jewel of South America. "Oh,
Paraguay, my favorite country in the continent!" said Laura
López, the longtime *Time* bureau chief for the whole of South
and Central America. She liked it? "I love it—the way you'd
love an orphan, or a bird with a broken foot." Paraguay was
something of an Ur-land, untamed, undeveloped, abandoned
by history, wood-paneled streetcars still clattering through its
streets, and electricity and running water arriving only a president ago. "It's a crazy country, wistful and surreal and forlorn,"
said a highly engaging American journalist who had lived there
for three years. "But it's magical—like Macondo in Gabriel
García Márquez." "The air is so pure," added her husband, a
Spanish writer. "And the streets are full of orange trees and
jacarandas and lapachos. When you arrive in Stroessner Airport,
you feel as if you are in one of the last corners of the world."

The sinister stories had been burnished by legend, the
woman went on. "But they never have mass slaughters in Paraguay the way they do in Chile and Argentina." Recently, she
pointed out, they'd even extradited two Argentine kidnappers.
Paraguay, in a sense, was like Rip Van Winkle after only twenty
winks. "And if Asunción's sleepy," she went on, "the rest of the
country's in a coma." Was there anything to do there? "Well,
you can go to the Jardín de la Cerveza [Garden of Beer] and
see women dancing with jugs on their heads." With that, she
ran out of suggestions. Then she perked up again. "Oh, and
they do have great hammocks there. Wonderful hammocks.
You see them hanging up on the main road out of town." "Yes,"
said her husband. "Excellent hammocks."

. . .

Leaving the Gran Hotel, I decided to move to the Oasis Hostel, its name translated into Korean outside its entrance. The Oasis was a curious place. Just inside its firmly double-bolted doors were several color pictures of Brazil—taken from a *Playboy* spread and concentrating on the country's topless beauties; on the opposite wall was a huge map of Argentina. Nearby was a series of formal snapshots of a Korean couple on their wedding day, in black tie and white gown, and beside them—quite a coup, I thought—an entire brochure on Paraguay aimed at a Korean audience (and centered around a strong-looking woman in a director's chair whom the brochure identified as "Producer Kim"). There were also, in the entrance hall, some photos, snipped from Korean fashion magazines, of bedroom sets in Seoul department stores.

I passed through this unlikely gallery, down a narrow alley-way, past another fortress of a door, and into a filthy courtyard. There I found a basketball hoop and a broken-down washing machine. A few plants were feebly protruding from some Nescafé bottles, and a body-length mirror announced at its top, "Christ is coming." In the middle of the courtyard stood a very large Korean teenage girl with a yapping dog on a leash.

She stared at me with little joy. "How many hours?" "Just one night, please." She looked at me blankly and tried again. "How many hours?" "Hours? I don't know. Maybe twenty-five, twenty-six." This was too much for her. Padding over to a red telephone, she picked it up, and I heard furious cries of "*Appa, Appa* . . ." Daddy apparently applied a tonic to her wounds, and she gloomily returned to our discussion, leading me off to a tiny room and fastening the dog to the door handle. The room consisted of a sagging bed, a table, and a trash can. "Do you have anything else?" I asked. She looked at me phlegmatically, then flip-flopped back to the red phone. "*Appa, Appa* . . ."

Again Daddy worked his rare magic, and she put the phone down and led me to another room. This one consisted of a sagging bed, a table, a trash can, and one entire wall covered with flesh-colored pictures, many of them poster size, of girls in every conceivable position — sunny side up, over easy, languid in French lace. In the middle of the porno shots was a replica of the Korean flag and a picture of a Korean girl, relatively modest in a chemise. Thinking this preferable to another suite we had passed, which came decorated with pictures of male heartthrobs and some faded Kyongju beauties, I instantly accepted.

As I was making myself comfortable in my new home, I began to see what services it provided. One three-foot pinup, featuring a girl climbing some stairs without benefit of underwear, was scribbled over with hearts and proclamations: "Nidi and Luis made love all night long 15-11-91." "Ramon Dermidio Iriquera and Rosa Catalino Gill made love here 1991–1992." On the back of the door, in a fit of graphomania, perhaps, Nidi and Luis had added: "Nidi and Luis here consolidated, mutually, their love." It was, in its way, a historic site.

Just as I was taking all this in, there came a knock on the door. It was *Appa* ("Daddy," as I now thought of him), my smiling host, a few furtive Paraguayan couples shuffling in and out of rooms behind him. He came in and blurted out something unintelligible about his life in Singapore. I responded with nonsensical protestations of my devotion to Korea. He asked me to give him some money—twenty-six hours' worth, at an hourly rate—and I assured him that I was a friend for life. Then he lurched into a brief discussion of the Olympic Games and some fairly searching questions about my marital status. Disconcerted, it seemed, by my replies, he suddenly looked deranged. *"Pooky-pooky no quieres?"* (Don't you want some pooky-pooky?) I looked at him dumbfounded. *"Chicas,"* he added, *"hay."* (Chicks are available.) Whether or not this was an invitation or a mere statement of fact, I decided not to ask whether Continental breakfast was also an offer.

The Koreans are, in fact, a highly visible, if somewhat shadowy, presence in modern Paraguay, subject of many rumors. ("There are 30,000 Koreans in the city," one boy in Asunción told me. "More than 1,200,000 Koreans here," another boy in Asunción said.) Some are here in hopes of migrating to the U.S. (since the quota from Paraguay is more accommodating than that from South Korea), some are here mostly to put their export-import skills to use in a country most notable for its lassitude. In either case, whole parts of the capital are flavored now with kimchi and decorated with signs for tae kwon do academies, Korean billiard halls, places like the Gimnasio Han Kwok. You can eat at *bulgogi* parlors here or at a place advertised—in Korean—as "Donald Kentucky Chicken." The Kims take up more than a column in the Asunción phone book, and shops are full of Lees with curly blond locks. Theirs is not a very welcoming community, however. When I went, my third night in town, into a Korean-run Japanese restaurant, I had not even sat down before the proprietor came up, asked me where I came from, and—when I said India—showed me the door.

Disappointed, I went into the Hidalgo Pizza Parlor down the street. A girl with a Korean frame, a half-Korean face, and sandy light-brown hair accosted me at the entrance but looked too terrified to throw me out. Reluctantly, she led me to a table next to a picture of Jesus and as far as possible from a gaggle of young Korean girls hiding their mouths with their hands. Luckily, they knew nothing of my interest in the works of Kim Il Sung.

The Koreans, though, are only one element in the improbable Paraguayan stew. One of the other main ingredients is simple, gaudy affluence. Drive down the length of Avenida

Mariscal López and you pass stores shaped like castles, car showrooms dressed in four-color neon, mansions made up to resemble the White House, Arabian castles, and Tara from *Gone with the Wind*. Up and down the cars prowl on Saturday nights, in one never-ending stream, past ice cream parlors offering "dietetic" snacks, past tanning centers and solaria. Much of the city, in fact, feels as if it were decorated by Judith Krantz: the streets are lined with hand-painted copies of famous Benetton and Calvin Klein ads, and everywhere you go you see familiar names—Sony, Burberry, Eastern Airlines; Lloyds Bank, Visa, Hyundai. Even the villages in the Brand-Name Republic are draped in Wranglers ads, and a huge banner hangs above the main street in the lakeside resort of San Bernardino: LUCKY STRIKE WISHES YOU A HAPPY SUMMER.

It is often said that the border between San Diego and Tijuana (and continuing along) is the only place on earth where the first world meets the third. The same claim could be made, however, for Avenida Brasil in Asunción, which divides this abandoned bastard child of Tijuana and La Jolla down the middle: on one side, the bargain-basement commotion of downtown; on the other, the jasmine-scented quiet of the mansions. What can one say about a city where the four-star hotels offer no direct-dial phone service—even within Asunción—while the taxis are Mercedeses? Where women carrying baskets of fruit on their heads walk past ice cream parlors that accept eleven international credit cards? Where the per capita income is half that of Mexico, yet twenty-first-century arcades abound? At the very least, it seems fair to say that Asunción enjoyed a radical face-lift in the seventies, when billions of dollars poured into the town from President Stroessner's construction deals—and it now seems only fitting that the main features of the suburbs are "facial" salons, makeup parlors, and plastic surgeons.

At the very least too, Paraguay seems to live by laws (or

no laws) of its own. Officially, the country claims only 34,000 passenger cars, about as many as Suriname (Brazil, by comparison, has 14 million, or 400 for every one in Paraguay). In a country full of two-car garages, whose streets are jammed with Volkswagens and Peugeots, this is a little strange.

Now I understand, I thought, what people mean when they talk of wealth as "obscene," as I cruised one day along Avenida Generalísimo Franco with an affluent Paraguayan, amidst nouveau mansions and Ralph Lauren kids, their BMW's disappearing behind electronic gates. "These people are rich," I said, trying not to look at the ugly scar across my young host's hand. "Not rich," he said sagely. "But they know how to take it." Soon he was pointing out sites of local interest: this was the house where Stroessner's son lived (the gay son, not the drug addict), this was the house where the general sold passports. "Every cent of highway tax, every penny of gasoline tax," he said, with some relish, "went straight into President Stroessner's personal bank account. Coca-Cola alone brought him forty thousand dollars a day in the summer." The minister of education, he went on, had diligently raised funds for seven hundred schools around the country, none of which existed; one colonel had been hired entirely to find nubile schoolgirls for the president.

All of this has ostensibly changed, in the era of President Rodríguez. Thus the walls are alive now with signs crying. "Enough repression of the *campesinos!*" and "Long live the struggle of the peoples of Iraq and Palestine!" and "Busch is an assassin!" And the newspapers seethe with discussions of a new constitution, the legalization of abortion, and the importance of a people's voice. Che Guevara is almost as ubiquitous today as the Marlboro Man. Yet a country whose heroes are all military tyrants is not ideally suited to democracy. The opposition, during the Stroessner days, used famously to sip maté at "demonstrations," to invite their government tails to come to the movies with them, and to wait for foreign journalists to tell them what to shout. If you visited the opposition leader's house, I was told, you would find a few men in ill-fitting suits, sipping iced maté and saying nothing. Come back three days later, and the same men would be in the same seats, sipping the same pipes. Occasionally, a fly would land, and someone would swat it away.

One day in Asunción, I saw a bright banner above the cathedral. "We too," it proclaimed in red and blue, inviting people to come to a rally outside the church to discuss the new constitution, at 8:00 p.m. on Thursday. At 8:00 p.m. on Thursday, the rally consisted of myself, looking somewhat bewildered, alone in a light rain.

"There are good politicians, yes," a seemingly liberal man assured me. "But the trouble is, a good politician has many enemies. A bad politician is ringed with friends." This man supported abortion and was opposed to the dictates of the Church. But he also supported dictatorship. "We need a strong government here," he said. "If there isn't one, there is only chaos. And if we have a civilian president, there's nothing but trouble with the military." The general feeling in Paraguay seemed to be one of *"Plus ça change . . ."* The Colorado Party men were still shouting. "Long live Stroessn—I mean, Rodríguez!" and the phone book still listed three Alfredo Stroessners.

I could not help dusting off a few of my apprehensions when I went to the Jardín Botánico, formerly an estate of the presidential Lopezes and now filled with the saddest and thinnest elephants and tigers I have ever seen. ("The little zoo," says the *South American Handbook*, in its inimitably tight-lipped way, "has inspired some unfavourable comments.") Around them were groups of children held together by circles of string behind their backs, and moving from cage to cage in what seemed to be portable cages of their own.

Nearby, in the Museum of Natural History, I finally cracked, amidst its hundreds of beetles and spiders pinned up in elaborate patterns on the wall, its staring pumas and stuffed albatross, its six-hundred-year-old preserved corpses, its skulls and its snakes like homunculi in jars. It looked like the workplace of some demented Frankenstein, and I could not help but think back to the stories of Dr. Mengele, who famously kept rows upon rows of eyes pinned up on his wall.

Yet such macabre scenes are in many respects the exception in Paraguay. The people here are generally amiable and attractive, and nicely turned out, if only because clothes and cosmetics are so inexpensive in this tax-free zone (even the schoolgirls here wear Dior and Worth). The license plates on the Alfas and Chevys, in the American way, give nicknames to every city— "Spiritual Capital," "Heroic City," "The Frontier of Friendship," "The Young and Happy City"—and the main post office is a lovely colonial building, with rooms radiating out from a sunlit, fountained Andalusian courtyard and upstairs, one of the sweetest views in the capital (not to mention a bust of Marshal López at its center and pictures of him around the walls). Bank tellers walk down the street with the straight-backed dignity of applicants for the Paraguayan Bottle Dance. Paraguay is not without its shady charms.

And there is something engagingly unpretentious about the place's openness and its apparent freedom from illusions about itself: the aerobics show I watched on TV seemed to be called "Kleppomania," and a jeans store (offering, as they all do, "Instant Personal Credit") called itself, nicely, "Credi-billy." Though a few cunningly angled photos present Asunción as a thoroughly modern city full of skyscrapers, the truth of the matter is that there are only about five or six high-rises in the entire place and they are topped by signs for Marlboro, Lucky Strike, and Philips.

The governing principle of Paraguay, indeed, seems to be one of languid illegality, and the country shambles along with an inimitable kind of slow-motion hustle—quick kills played out at a tropical pace. For all the talk of *negocios*, Paraguay has none of the huckster's usual energy or determination, none of the con man's tenacity; by Saturday noon, all the money changers have gone home for the weekend, and the bankers are drifting into the No Problems bar. The guidebooks always point out that offices here open at 7:00 a.m. or even 6:00; what they neglect to mention is that the banks, for example, close at 11:00. This is the land of the four-day siesta. If there were a prize for the world's least persistent touts, Paraguay would surely win lying down. ("How much for this?" "Twenty thousand guaraní!" "I'll give you five thousand." "Okay.") In Paraguay, there's no business like slow business.

For me, then, the essence—the spiritual heart—of Asunción was the Plaza Uruguaya, a leafy park just a few blocks from the center. Old men sipped maté under trees, and younger men pitched coins along the sidewalk. Hot-pants girls winked lazily at every passerby, next to the statue of the Virgin donated by the Lions Club of Asunción. A small crowd formed to watch men playing checkers in the shade.

On one side of the square stood the quaint yellow railway station, whose construction, like much else, had been cut short by the War of the Triple Alliance. A sign proudly reported that it was the first train station in South America—neglecting to add that it was now the last to receive steam engines. In the empty portico outside the station, raspy voiced old women of nineteen and twenty hissed "Pssst!" at every unaccompanied male, while girls under umbrellas flagged down passing cars with lottery tickets. Within the plaza itself there were two huge transparent tubes that looked like cellular greenhouses made of cellophane. Inside were stacks of books—though this seemed an unlikely spot for literateurs—with titles like *Absolution for Hitler?*, *My Cat Speaks* ("A Book of Mediumistic conversations between a human being and two cats"), and *Read the Future in Grounds of Coffee*. The works of Lobsang Rampa, the "Tibetan lama" later exposed as a fraudulent Englishman, seemed especially popular in Paraguay.

I took to spending a few moments each day in the square, watching the world go by—or not do so. The plaza seemed like the *echt* Paraguay, fragrant with the blessings of a place that time has left behind.

From the Oasis I moved onto a NASA bus for a trip into the Chaco, the vast, impenetrable scrubland that takes up two-thirds of all Paraguay, a place so hellish that the average temperature (allowing for many 75° days) is 98° Fahrenheit, a place so primitive that a wild hog believed to be extinct since the Pleistocene era was found there less than a generation ago. On the bus, I and the driver were the only ones without blond heads. *Hausfrauen* with yellow buns were chattering away in *Plattdeutsch* with old German men in farmers' caps. A family of four very blond Californians was sitting in one row transporting boxes of Frosted Flakes to fellow missionaries in the interior. The driver, in any case, was often not visible, except for his legs, which dangled in the aisle from a hole in the roof, where he was hacking down branches with an evil-looking machete. The Brazilian-made bus had symbols on its side of TV, Video, Music, Drinks, Playing Cards, and a WC. As far as I could see, it did have a WC. Still, it seemed the best vehicle to take: the other two daily buses arrived in the desolate Chaco at 2:00 a.m. and 3:30 a.m. respectively.

Within thirty minutes of leaving the capital, we were in oblivion: just trees, greenness, space, greenness, here and there a small white grave beside the road. We drove past the

Río Confuso, the town of Benjamin Aceval, the *departamento* of Presidente Hayes. There are wonderful birds in the Chaco—birds with transparent wings, birds with pink feathers, birds in the colors of Brazil. There is not much else. The population density here is less than one person per square kilometer.

As darkness fell, there was marginally less to see. Driving through the Chaco at night is like walking through the dark with your eyes shut. About sixty kilometers from the last light, the bus might stop and two elderly Germans might get off and disappear into the dark. Then the bus would resume its straight-line path. "When can we get off?" bawled one of the missionaries' sons. Are we having fun yet? The Chaco is not an ideal honeymoon location.

Finally, after nine o'clock, we arrived at Filadelfia, the main Mennonite settlement in Colonia Fernheim. I got out and started walking down the huge, unpaved red road, broad as the Champs-Élysées. "Filly," as the Californians affectionately called it, is like an empty, one-lane, red-mud version of the Wild West. On all sides, you can see the town end and the nothingness begin. There is a used-car lot here and a Toyota showroom--this is, after all, still Paraguay—but not much else. One pickup truck; three straw-haired boys on Yamahas.

I wandered into the Hotel Florida, on the corner of Avenida Hindenburg and Calle Unruh, just two doors down from the *Reisebüro*, and was greeted by a very polite young Uruguayan boy who looked like Boris Becker. *"Kann ich diese Zeitung nehmen?"* I asked him, "Of course," he said, in flawless English. "But will that be enough for you?" On the walls of the hotel were daily rainfall tables (whole months passed by without a single marking, and then, on some days, it said 204, 131, 189). There was also a map of the area: the Chaco is so deserted that the maps show every house and shop.

I went into the courtyard to have dinner and met two young

Brits who had lost their way, on their bicycles, in the middle of the Bolivian part of the Chaco. We established that we were from the same country, and then ate at opposite sides of the empty garden.

What the Mennonites have achieved in this inhospitable "Green Hell" is quite remarkable. ("In the summer, the temperature's about one twenty-five," a man in Asunción had told me. "But with the humidity, of course, it feels much higher.") When first the German settlers arrived, fleeing Russian Communism in 1930, they found an ungodly wilderness peopled only by a few Indians, and swarming with poisonous snakes. Many caught typhoid and died. Two years after they arrived, the Chaco War broke out all around them. Yet somehow they hung on to erect an astonishingly clean and well-managed community, with its own schools, buses, laws, and enormous cooperative stores. The supermarket in Filadelfia was spotless and better stocked than a store in Orange County and offered Japanese Super Gummi candies, Chinese Perfect Cube boxes, Jordache jeans, and tapes of Fips Asmussen. Nearby, a Christian bookstore ("The Messenger") sold Indian statues of turtles and owls, and a video store promised James Bond and Mad Max, as well as special tapes in German, of the Bombing of Baghdad and the Paris-Dakar rally.

But the most exciting thing to do in Filadelfia, for me, was simply to watch the Mennonite women clean my room every morning. A task force of three stormed into the small, immaculately maintained chamber, scrubbing floors, beating rugs, picking up shoes, whisking off wastebaskets and then storming out three minutes later, leaving the place born again.

My first morning in town, I went for a ride through the red-rutted emptiness with the proprietor of the hotel, a wonderfully hospitable Mennonite named Hartmut Wohlgemuth, accompanied by a sweet-smiling young Paraguayan proselyte. We bumped over tire-muddied paths, the roads around as empty as airstrips (which often they are), the cries of *"Danke schön"* as frequent as in a Cuban police station. "Before, the Indians could not sleep at night," my host explained. "They believed in spirits, ghosts, things almost satanic. They were afraid of the night, of things that moved in the dark. It was terrible. Now they believe in Jesus. And this is better. Whoever you are— Paraguayan, Brazilian, German, Indian—you can believe in Jesus and find salvation. I am not just saying this. It is the truth."

Not everyone here could keep up with such fervor. "It is a big problem," Herr Wohlgemuth admitted. "The young do not want to live like this. They want excitement, the modern life. They want money. They want drink." Did many of them marry the Indians? "Not really," he said, and then went on, with characteristic straightforwardness, "They have sexual relations, of course. But marry, no."

We drove into Indian settlements famously appointed with basketball courts, prayer halls, and Bible schools: they looked like rough drafts of the Mennonite communities. "Some Indians have TV's, radios," Herr Wohlgemuth informed me. "Some even have cars." "Do they want all this?" "Yes. They all want them." A few Indians clattered past on a horse-drawn cart, like latter-day replicas of the early Mennonites; others played volleyball, or stood inertly by their huts in Minnesota Vikings T-shirts. We got out, and an aged Indian man, in lucid Spanish, gave us an account of the missionary's life. "El Señor was hit by a bow and arrow. The arrow went into his side. There was no blood. Three hours later, he was dead."

We got back into the pickup, and my beaming host, patting me on the back, pointed out serpents, *tuca-tucas*, and, mostly, doves. I thought it might be imprudent to ask him about the Ache Indians, a small Stone Age tribe of hunters and gatherers who, according to many reports, have been virtually eliminated by missionaries. (Norman Lewis, only a few years ago, wrote of a man selling his own son for seventy-five cents, down from the going rate of five dollars.) Better, I thought, to discuss the most famous reported settler among the Mennonites.

"Do you know Dr. Mengele?" "Mengele? No! People say that he lived among the Mennonites, but that is a lie! A complete lie! He was never here, never! They found his bones in São Paulo!" "Yes," piped up the Paraguayan from the back seat, unschooled yet in the party line. "He was with another group of Mennonites, in another part of Paraguay. He was a doctor among the insane." "Another group?" said Herr Wohlgemuth, a little taken aback. "Really?" "Yes. He was a doctor before." "But a rustic doctor only." "He was a friend of Stroessner," the boy from Asunción went on. I was about to ask what this said about Stroessner—the madman responsible for up to 400,000 deaths was said to be the president's personal physician—but then the smiling boy went on: "He was a good man, Stroessner, a very good man. He returned to Paraguay last week."

Herr Wohlgemuth was the perfect host, a thoroughly likable soul who roared with joy when he saw a motorcyclist do a wheelie. He stopped in Lomo Plata, the largest Mennonite settlement in Menno, and he bought us ice creams in a Mennonite shop decorated with posters about how cholera could be caught from ice cream. "It is difficult," he said, now contemplative. "Between our culture and the Indians' there is a Mediterranean." That night, he screened for me a video of the Indians singing a hymn, in Spanish, to the tune of "Red River Valley."

When I retuned to the capital, everything was still ambling along in its state of lazy illegitimacy. A black magician was holding court in the Plaza of the Heroes, performing tricks before a huge circle of admirers with a spitting snake and a reptile in a box. The camera artists were doing a roaring trade snapping prints of excited young girls in from the countryside, and touts in UNIVERSITY OF FLORIDA COLLEGE OF LAW T-shirts were palming bank notes above shirts that said OAKLAND ATHLETICS 1954 WORLD CHAMPIONS (BASKETBALL WORLD SERIES). The Cine Victoria had a new double bill: *Deep Throat II* and *The Night of Penetrations*.

In the Plaza Uruguaya, the same girls in the same polka-dot dresses were standing against the same trees. Occasionally, they snuggled up to distracted-looking businessmen on park benches and talked in numbers ("Fifteen thousand." "Ten!" "Why not fifteen?"), before shuffling off together to the nearby Casa Reina, or House of Queens. I asked a girl if she was not worried about AIDS. It was a lie, she said, it didn't exist (and in Paraguay, you could almost believe it: anything could be true on this distant planet).

At night a blood-red fountain began to play in the Plaza of the Heroes, and children went round it solemnly on tricycles. The parking space outside the Hotel Guarani was still reserved for the Embassy of South Africa. On TV, messages about cholera were flashing across the screen during advertisements for the Miss Universe contest. Booming above me, from the "Dancing Restaurant," there came the sound of a band doing "My Way." The next day was a national holiday—Workers' Day—which was a strange notion in a land where 60 percent of the people have no real work at all.

Yet for all the slow-business as usual, I could see why so many visitors had a soft spot for Paraguay. For there are very few shadows in Paraguay, and the capital at least is one of the safest places on the continent. In a country where crookedness is above ground and official ("Legalize Crime" might almost be the national motto: "Just Say Yes!"), people have more lucrative ways to redistribute income than by taking advantage of visitors.

One could, in fact, make a Wildean case, after seeing Paraguay, for saying that if crime were made legal (as it is here), petty crime—pickpocketing and mugging and assault—would be all but eliminated. The only things I was robbed of in Paraguay were my malign preconceptions: I never looked over my shoulder here, or thought twice about taking a walk, or left my valuables in the hotel, as I would have to do in fun-loving, free-and-easy, murderous Rio. At night, there was a policeman—or a prostitute—on every street corner, keeping the peace in a kind of way.

Before I left Paraguay, I returned to the Gran Hotel. The golden kids of the generals were practicing their forehands, and the babies were squawking and whistling like birds. "Too many babies," whispered the friendly receptionist, the cosmopolitan daughter of a diplomat, and an amateur historian. "But what can we do? We cannot refuse them rooms. Maybe we can set up a special room for them where they will not disturb the other guests?"

"Yes," I said. "After all, this is a place with a special history."

"No it isn't."

"I just mean Madama Lynch and all that."

"She never lived here."

"What?"

"I tell you, I don't know where that rumor started. It's a lie! The truth must be told!"

There was a long and uncomfortable silence.

"This house belonged to an Italian family. *They* lived here. Madama Lynch lived near the Jardín Botánico. I think they just started that story to bring in guests."

Fact or fiction, truth or gossip? Who could tell? History, like everything else, was on special discount here in the orphaned land.

FIVE THOUSAND MILES FROM ANYWHERE

Start with the light. Everything starts with the light here.

In the hour before nightfall, what Hollywood calls the "magic hour," the buildings in Australia start to glow with an unearthly light, and the gold-touched clouds look like something Blake might have imagined in his highest moments. The sky becomes a canvas on which absent gods are doodling: over here, patches of tropical blue; over there, shafts of silver slanting through the slate-gray clouds; everywhere, double rainbows arcing over gray Victorian monuments and avenues of palms. Yet this is hardly a warming scene. Rather, the Australian twilight has the same chilly strangeness, the same otherworldly calm—the same off-the-edge-of-the-earthliness—as Iceland in midsummer: a cold and science-fictive beauty. And as the night begins to descend, it seems as if the land is reclaiming itself, and Australia is more than ever a place emptied out of people, some dark, elemental presences awakened behind the placid surfaces of its newborn world.

The light in Australia is like nothing else on earth—as befits, perhaps, a country that feels as if it has fallen off the planet. "Australia's like an open door with the blue beyond," wrote D. H. Lawrence. "You just walk out of the world and into Australia." And the startled intensity of the heavens hints at all the weird paradoxes of this young old land of sunny ironists, a British California caught between a world it has abandoned and one it has yet to colonize. In the vast open blueness of Australia, the only presiding authority, it often seems, is the light.

Australia is, of course, the definitive—perhaps the ulti-mate—*terra incognita*, its very name derived from the Latin phrase *terra australis incognita*, or unknown land of the south. Captain Cook first bumped into the land of anomalies while trying to observe a transit of the planet Venus. And even today the world's largest island seems to occupy a huge open space in the mind, beyond the reach of our sights. Australia, for one thing, borders nothing and is on the way to nowhere. It feels, in every sense, like the last place on earth. Colonized originally by the British as a place for posthumous lives—a kind of Alcatraz on an epic scale—Australia has always seemed the natural set-ting for postapocalyptic imaginings, from Lawrence's utopian visions to Nevil Shute's nuclear wasteland to the haunted death-scape of *Mad Max*.

What little we know of this tabula rasa, moreover, has gener-ally sounded like fiction. "In Australia alone," as Marcus Clarke wrote, "is to be found the Grotesque, the Weird, the strange scribblings of Nature learning to write." The flattest and driest of the continents defies all the laws of probability with its natu-ral—or unnatural—wonders: not just the world's only egg-laying mammals (the echidna and the duckbill platypus) but the wombat and the wallaby, the koala, the kangaroo, the kooka-burra and the quokka. A land of extremes, it is also one of inversions, an antipodean place where Christmas is celebrated in midsummer and the water goes the wrong way down the drain, a looking-glass world in which trees lose their bark but not their leaves, and crows, it is said, fly backwards (to keep the dust from their eyes). Even the country's social origins are the stuff of Restoration comedy, a down-underworld in which convicts were known as "government men" and thieves were appointed as magistrates—less the Promised than the Threatened Land.

Yet it is in the nature of Lonely Places to attract people, in large part because of their loneliness, and in this, the year of its Bicentenary, Providence has conspired with promotion to render Australia suddenly ubiquitous. Sports fans watch Pat Cash at Wimbledon and the America's Cup dominate the headlines; Americans flock in record numbers to sit at the feet of the new Paul Bunyan, Paul Hogan in *Crocodile Dundee;* MTV gave nearly all its recent awards to an Aussie band with the typically over-the-top name of INXS; and the highest literary award in the English-speaking world, the Booker Prize in Britain, went this autumn to the Australian novelist Peter Carey.

Two million foreigners are visiting Australia this year, to take in a "shriek opera," a camel race, and the other unlikely props of an intensely laid-back Bicentenary. Yet the greatest reason of all for Australia's sudden appeal is, in the end, the very thing that has outlawed it for so long: the tyranny of distance. Suddenly, people are realizing that Australia is so far from the world that it is the ideal place for people who wish to get away from the world, do nothing, and watch others do the same. The quietness, and unhurried spaciousness, of the Empty Continent can make one feel as if one has all the time in the world— indeed, as if time and the world have both been annulled: "rush hour" is not a term in common currency here. And though irreverence is an Australian article of faith, the most urbanized society on earth (70 percent of Aussies live in eight major cities) is increasingly endowed with all the gentrified accoutrements of a brunch culture: hotels so untouched they feel like resorts, towns that are drawing-board models of clean lines and open spaces, people who are devoted to life, liberty, and the pursuit of happiness. Not the least of the ironies governing a nation whose founding fathers were convicts is, in fact, that it is now most noted for its air of freedom, safety, and civic order.

Australia's achievement, in that sense, is to conflate, or overturn, the very notions of urban and pastoral: its biggest city enjoys 342 days of sunshine a year; and even drizzly, Victorian Melbourne has a hundred beaches in its vicinity. The pastel-perfect new hotels are less than a day away from barrier reefs, crocodile forests, and sere spaces: even the high-flying elegance of Sydney's Opera House is shadowed by the rooted, runic magic of Ayers Rock. Some of the popular myths about Australia may be little more than myths (a visitor can spend three weeks in the country without seeing a 'roo or meeting a Bruce), but some are undoubtedly true. They do play lagerphones here, made entirely of beer-bottle caps; the long *a* is an endangered species; and in the "Red Centre," fat flies do drop like men.

Though Australia appears on the map of *Gulliver's Travels*, nobody has determined whether it is Brobdingnag, Lilliput, or the land of the Yahoos. The overwhelming fact about the place is its size: cattle stations the size of Massachusetts, an Outback so vast that doctors make their house calls by plane; a land so outstretched that Perth, capital of a state ten times the size of Great Britain, is as close to the nearest big city, Adelaide, as London is to Leningrad. The terms themselves insist on grandeur: the Great Dividing Range, the Great Barrier Reef, the Great Artesian Basin; the Great Western Plateau, the Great Ocean Road, and the Great Victoria Desert.

Yet what strikes one most forcibly upon landing in Australia is, in a sense, how small it is, how empty; here, one feels, is a small town built on a giant scale, like Montana blown up to the size of a continent. Even the cities resound with an eerie quietness: a third of central Melbourne is parkland; in the capital of Canberra, kangaroos hop across the golf courses; and even in Sydney itself there is no sense of urgency or pressure. On a mild spring morning in the heart of the city, there is nothing but palm trees, a soft breeze, and the song of birds. Here one can hardly imagine, let alone keep up with, a world that seems more than a day away.

And though Sydney is technically larger than Los Angeles County or Greater London, it is the focus for an air of neglectedness that haunts much of Australia, its sense of having been finished (or half finished) only yesterday. The solitary skyscrapers in the city are huddled in an unprepossessing bunch beside the harbor; its Greenwich Village, Paddington, lies mostly along a single street; and its center of red-lit nightlife, Kings Cross, can be seen in a mere ten minutes. The sense of an uninhabited, an inchoate land continues through the suburbs. Drive along the Pacific Highway (a modest, two-lane road), and you pass through town after lonely town of cheerful toy-box buildings, bright against a dizzy blueness, a depleted succession of cheerful one-street, one-story townships in silent Edward Hopper rows. Here, in a sense, is Rockwell's America—or, more precisely, Reagan's: a placid, idealized small-town world of village greens and local churches, an oasis of sunlit optimism suspended in a sleepy haze of laissez-faire conservatism and lazy tolerance.

The apogee of this sense of bright tranquillity is, of course, the synthetic capital, Canberra, a leafy, landscaped monument to spotlessness that even the Duke of Edinburgh called "a city without a soul" (though in fact it feels less like a city than a work of art: a stunning sculpture garden on a giant scale, its government offices and embassies placed like so many architectural conceits amidst its huge and empty lawns). Canberra is a place where nothing plays except the fountains—it has the haunting quietness of a de Chirico landscape of long shadows and lonely colonnades, a Lonely Place institutionalized. Yet at the same time, there is no denying the beauty of this Forest Lawn of designer splendor, its clean horizons undisturbed even by TV antennae or garden fences (both of which are banned). And the sense of uncreatedness that informs much of Australia here finds its pinnacle in the spacey new Parliament House. Its seats prettily designed in the pale greens and pinks of gum trees, its chambers flooded with natural light, the new center of government looks like nothing so much as another of the country's sparkling new hotels.

This disarming sense of openness extends, not surprisingly, to the citizenry, and Australians often seem as sunny and breezy as the world around them. Taxi drivers, airline officials, and waiters go about their work in shorts. Conversations are as common as people, and just about as casual. The prime minister here is a "bloke" known as Bob, who is still admired for drinking his way into the *Guinness Book of World Records*; a local Scientology proselytizer is a bearded man who leans against a wall and drawls lackadaisically, "Excuse me, mate."

"Everyone is happy-go-lucky, and one couldn't *fret* about anything if one tried," complained the congenitally fretful D. H. Lawrence in a letter back home. Mohawked boys may chew their girlfriends' lips in the beery rockabilly bars of Melbourne, and Australia may still exalt the outcast, but generally this seems an exceptionally unaggressive place: the graffiti on Melbourne's picturesque streetcars is artistically applied at government behest. Here, remember, is a country that did not have to work or fight for independence but simply backed into it, a little halfheartedly—and then let circumstance turn the Fatal Shore into the Lucky Country.

In Australia's laid-back sense of come-as-you-are palliness, many foreign observers have found a model of democracy in action, a natural kind of Whitmanic fraternalism free of ideological baggage. Calling a spade a spade is a national habit, after all, and nothing seems to anger the Australian but pretension. Though Lawrence may have been merely being Lawrence when he claimed that Australians were such natural democrats that they did not even like to go upstairs, it is certainly true that a visitor is more likely to be called "mate" than "sir."

Yet if Australians' customs are often as unbuttoned as those of the American West, their manners are generally a little more reserved; touched with *le vice anglais* of self-containment, theirs is still a place of semidetached men in semidetached houses. And even though its feeling of space and ease, like its gold rush past and its sense of limitless future, gives Australia a somewhat Californian air, it feels more provisional, more pressureless than the frontier states of America, less troubled by introspection or ambition. Here, in fact, is a world that makes California seem positively frantic by comparison. In his novel *Bliss*, a typically Australian compound of irony, fancy, and profanity, Peter Carey shrewdly depicts his homeland as a mythic Eden "on the outposts of the American Empire . . . [with] business more or less done in the American style, although without quite the degree of seriousness the Americans liked."

Australia, moreover, still holds to its fondness for the piratical, a sense that distinction lies not in the flaunting but in the flouting of refinement. The country delights in the marginal, glories in its freedom from convention, is determined to be different. There is a store in Sydney (as in London) exclusively for left-handers, and the sign in the Melbourne bookshop canvasses members for a *Lost in Space* club. And Australia's traditional images of rowdy nonconformity are still in constant evidence. The larrikin lives on in the eleven-year-old busker in earrings and rattail haircut who plays drinking songs in front of Sydney harbor while his Fagin looks on from the shadows; the convict and prospector are remembered in the dark humor of the names that overbrood the landscape—Lake Disappointment, Cape Grim, Double Crossing Creek; and the ocker asserts his skeptical down-to-earthiness with the bumper sticker EVERYBODY NEEDS TO BELIEVE IN SOMETHING. I BELIEVE I'LL HAVE ANOTHER BEER. In this seriously macho culture, you see more men in earrings than anywhere else—less a statement of fashion, one senses, than a badge of defiant rebelliousness.

To some extent, too, the myths of frontier still animate the culture. Many young Australians continue to take off around the world, treating jobs as way stations and anywhere as home, while many retirement couples take to their mobile homes and circumnavigate the land. And though the country feels less restless than America, it is surely just as mobile. Everywhere there are dreams of long horizons: a concierge is studying Chinese to expand his prospects; a cabbie is working sixty hours a week in the hope of visiting South America; a waiter at an exclusive French restaurant simply picks up his camera and guitar and heads off for a new life in the Outback.

Mike, a rugged, long-breeched man who runs a riding stable outside Melbourne, recalls how he came here alone on a boat at the age of fourteen, propelled by grand dreams awakened by Zane Grey. "There was a feeling that I could do nothing in England; and no matter how well I did at school, I could never go to university. That was just something that people like me didn't do. But over here, anything is possible. No way I could start up a place like this in England."

Besides, with its reverence for unorthodoxy and its sense of being away from it all, Australia remains an ideal retreat for odd men out. At times, in fact, one has the impression that it is less a culture than an aggregation of subcultures, a society of fringes—of surfers, cowboys, boozers, and hippies. Alternative life-styles are the norm in many places, and the prospect of starting a new life has natural appeal for those committed to

Rebirthing. The lush rolling hills known as the Rainbow Region, an hour east of the Gold Coast, have become a perfect haven for back-to-the-land purists and hypnotherapists, and the local bulletin board offers all the Oriental arts, from tai chi to tae kwon do. (The Breath of Life Relaxation and Healing Centre promises "Reiki healing" and "Lazaris videos"—all of this next to Woolworth's!) Still, mellowness here takes on a decidedly Aussie twang: "Shoplifting gives you bad karma!" advises a trendy Asian boutique in Sydney. "And if I catch you, I'll make sure you get it in this life—you Rat Fink! Sincerely, Sandi."

At the same time, Australia, like many a colony, has never entirely left behind the country that abandoned it here. As the relentlessly clever Tasmanian-born critic Peter Conrad points out in his half-autobiography, *Down Home*, Australians wistfully tried to assuage their homesickness by reinventing the motherland here—Tasmania alone has "a cliffless Dover, a beachless Brighton, an unindustrial Sheffield." A local newspaper may have no qualms about describing the visiting Duchess of York as "astonishingly frumpish," yet still her befreckled visage adorns at least three magazine covers in a single week. And even as the tattoo-and-bare-skin crowd is crowding in to see Mick Jagger (who once acted as the country's favorite outlaw, Ned Kelly) perform at the National Tennis Center, hundreds of well-behaved families are lining up to visit Prince Andrew's boat, docked down the coast in Tasmania.

In all these respects, as in many others, Australia still revels in the paradox of its mongrel origins, the contradictory features of a place of English institutions and American life-styles (reflected even in the name Crocodile Dundee—a Scotland in the wilderness!). And if modern Australia is often gazing over one shoulder at the land that gave it birth, it is looking over the other at the land it most resembles: here, after all, is a British parliamentary system with a Senate and a House of Representatives. The divided loyalties are everywhere apparent: in Hobart, the Doctor Syntax guesthouse is just down the street from Mister Pizza; in a Reptile World not far from Darwin, two snakes repose the vigorously contemporary and curiously Victorian names of Rocky and Rowena. While Melbourne high society dresses up in top hats and tails for the local version of Ascot, the Melbourne Cup, many others dress down—in almost nothing at all—to spoof the solemnity.

Of all the legacies of its English, and its castaway, roots, in fact, perhaps the strongest is the country's sardonic and seditious wit. Australia has a sly sense of irony that gives an edge to its sunshine, makes it something more than just a pretty face. That air of wry mischief is apparent in the Club Foote Cabaret, or the ad for a "Top Tourist Attraction" that features nothing but the photo of a sage-bearded man under the title "The Opal King." The comment in a museum's visitors' book is as dry as the Outback: "Could be worse." And the man who is being acclaimed as Australia's Woody Allen is a thirty-two-year-old writer-director whose name alone—Yahoo Serious—places him a fair distance away from the Bergman of the Upper West Side. Nothing, it seems, is sacred: at the Collins Baptist Church in Melbourne, Reverend Ham is discoursing on the theme "God is Parked Outside your Front Door."

In many ways, the country seems to mainstream, and mainline, its idiosyncrasies: the touristy stores around Sydney's refurbished Rocks area feature adorable koalas done up in convict suits, pineapples sporting shades, Punk Panda T-shirts. And the roadsides of Australia are lined with enormous absurdities: a fifteen-foot metal cheese, a thirty-foot dairy cow, a thirty-two-foot fiberglass banana. The little town of Mildura sells itself as the home of the most of the biggest, a title that apparently includes having the longest deck chair in the world, the longest bar, and—great apotheosis!—the largest talking Humpty-

Dumpty. Alice Springs hosts a regatta each year, in a dry river-bed, and Darwin responds with such inimitably Australian festivities as a Beer Can Regatta, the Froggolympics, and the World's Barefoot Mud Crab Tying championship.

Recently, the Northern Territorians have discovered that the biggest growth industry of all is in crocodilians. Arrive at Darwin Airport, and you will be greeted by Crocodile Attack Insurance policies and brochures describing Alligator Airlines, which runs float planes down to Bungle Bungle. Drive into town, and you will find Crocodile Motors, the Crocodile Lodge, croc pizza at Crocodile Corner, and stores selling nothing but croc bags, croc water pistols, huge inflatable crocs, and croc T-shirts (in forty different designs). The Sweethearts piano bar at the local casino serves—inevitably—"crocktails," and one life-size croc has been created entirely out of beer cans; on the road into Kakadu National Park, some shrewd entrepreneurs have even erected a twenty-foot tall crocodile, cruelly equipped with boxing gloves. Not long ago, the Four Seasons hotel chain opened up, nearby, the world's first hotel shaped entirely like a crocodile, a 750-foot, $11 million monstrosity with evil yellow eyes and a huge gray spine. When one croc decapitated a fisherman last year, in front of a transfixed group of tourists, it was rumored that a tour operator promptly demanded more of the same.

Thus Australians seem at once to play up, and play down, to tourist expectations; theirs is as much a subversive as a supplicant air. On a Qantas flight into Sydney, a cabin attendant mimes along with the safety announcement, while one of the tour guides at the Opera House is as floridly self-amusing as any guide this side of Key West. The Jolly Swagman show of Australiana in the quaintly renovated 150-year-old Argyle Tavern in Sydney suddenly causes its laughing visitors to blanch when it stages an actual sheep-shearing on stage, followed by an impromptu lecture from a bearded Bushman over his bald, still bleeding victim. And as a shuttle bus pulls out of Alice Springs train station, its passengers dazed from twenty-four hours in tiny compartments, the beefy driver unexpectedly bursts into tour-guide patter: "Directly in front of us," he begins, "we have the K mart."

This fondness for drollery, and its attendant suspicion of all stuffiness, breathes constant life and surprise into the country's culture. Folksingers stroll with guitars around the lovely main reading room of Adelaide's old Mortlock Library, and the country's museums are scarcely cathedrals of orthodoxy. The Hyde Park Barracks Museum in Sydney devotes an entire floor to plastic bags, embellished with videos of people banging bags together and a guide denoting "Points in Plastic History." The National Gallery in Melbourne fills one display case, rather surprisingly, with a pig's head and offers, in alarming proximity, specimens designated as "Lamb Brains," "Calves Livers" and "Spring Lamb Chops." (The stained-glass ceiling that is the museum's centerpiece can be appreciated only by visitors supine on the floor.) When the Opera House, financed largely by lotteries and partly by kissing contests, staged its first performance, koalas and kangaroos bounded across the stage in front of the visiting Queen.

It is common, of course, to hear people claim that Australian culture is a contradiction in terms: Bronte is a beach here, they say, and the country's unofficial national anthem, "Waltzing Matilda," was written by a man named Banjo. Certainly the feeling that the world lies outside the country's borders has propelled many rare minds to find themselves in exile: Germaine Greer, Clive James, and Robert Hughes all evince a uniquely Australian mix of erudition and iconoclasm, yet all are features now of the Anglo-American scene; and the brief wave of tasteful Masterpiece Movies that put Australia on the world's screens at the beginning of the eighties subsided when the directors of *Breaker Morant, Gallipoli,* and *The Devil's Playground* transported their Australian myths to America. Australians have so flexible a sense of home, perhaps, that they can make themselves at home anywhere.

Nonetheless, the culture still has a native vigor constantly quickened by its unforced sense of free speech. The Old Parliament House in Adelaide reserves an entire room that any group can take over for a month, and a bulletin board on which visitors respond to the displays set up by euthanasiasts, conservationists, or just plain Liberals. And the excellent Migration Museum around the corner likewise maintains a "Community Access Gallery." Far from sanitizing the country's rocky history of migration, moreover, the museum delivers some unpretty home truths ("Racist attitudes towards Asians have a very long history in Australia") and does not shy away from asserting that the aboriginals were "hunted and herded like animals." Provocative and hard-hitting, this is a fresh kind of art form: the museum as radical documentary.

The first-time visitor, indeed, may well be surprised at how conspicuous is the aboriginal presence. Though their numbers once sank to almost 60,000, the original guardians of the continent now constitute a subculture of more than 228,000, and many non-aboriginal Australians are aware that the usurpation of a people who regarded the land itself as their sacred text and mythology represents, in a very particular sense, a kind of desecration. It is this position that finds the Bicentenary most irrelevant. "Why celebrate two hundred years old when society here is forty thousand years old?" challenges a thoughtful young Australian. "And why call it our party when it should be theirs?"

The other most striking feature of Australia today is the prominence of the "New Australians," the latest wave of immigrants, who have turned cities like Melbourne into a clash of alien tongues as piquant and polyglot as New York, where nothing seems outlandish except standard English. The signs for public toilets in Melbourne are written in Greek (as well as English and Italian), churches solicit worshipers in Korean script, and when the Prostitutes Collective recently put out a multilingual pamphlet urging customers to use condoms, one of the tongues they employed was Macedonian. Though Australian voices still sound blond, their heads are increasingly dark: at the stately old Windsor Hotel in Melbourne, one of the last great relics of Victorian elegance, the maître d' is Vietnamese, the waiters are Sri Lankan, the owners are Indian, and the courtly man serving drinks comes from Bangladesh.

Inevitably, such developments have been somewhat tumultuous in a country whose leading magazine, as recently as 1960, ran with the slogan "Australia for the White Man." For decades isolation bred ignorance, and ignorance intolerance. Even today, the country whose ghost lurks at the edge of many a conversation in Australia is South Africa. "Australia is a very racist country," says a conservative English immigrant. "If you just scratch the surface, you come upon it. England's bad too, of course, but at least they've had to face up to the problem. Here it's still simmering."

The unease felt by some Australians as Vietnamese and Chinese have streamed down the golden brick road to Oz has only deepened as the new "Austr-aliens" have flourished through such imported virtues as seriousness and unrelenting hard work. For decades, as Donald Horne argued in *The Lucky Country*, his scathing attack on Aussie complacency, the country languished in a kind of lottery consciousness, content to believe that success was more the result of luck than of industry (in a single year, the estimated turnover from betting was three times the defense budget). Now, however, the determination of the immigrants, bolstered by the entrepreneurial energy of such controversial types as Rupert Murdoch and Alan Bond, has begun to invest Australia with a new sense of dynamism and to raise fresh questions about its identity as an Asian power. Twenty-four years after the publication of Horne's attack, the country may be less prosperous, but it is decidedly more promising.

Today, in many ways, Australia seems to reflect the eccentric ways of a Western European society set down in the middle of a Lonely Place: hotels as imaginatively designed as pavilions in some world's fair; cities that offer Balkan, Burmese, Mauritian, Uruguayan, and Seychellian cuisine; casinos that are typically down-home affairs where neither solemnity nor discretion is held in high regard ("Not a Poker Face in Sight," promises the Adelaide casino). Nearly all the heads in Australian bars are frothy, and tattooed bikers down 3.3-pint "stubbies" of Foster's in dusty outposts like the Humpty Doo Bar, where a bulletin board advertises pigs and a sign warns customers tersely, "Don't Ask for Credit as Refusal Often Offends." Australian entertainment, in fact, is nothing if not straightforward: a slim tourist brochure in Melbourne includes twenty-two full ads for escort agencies.

For the historically minded traveler, the main lure of the place may well be Tasmania, the oldest convict settlement after Sydney, and one of those out-of-the-way places that many people want to visit because of their vague sense that no one has visited them before. With its blustery skies and lowering, snow-capped Mount Wellington, Tasmania is in some respects an inversion of the mainland, itself an inversion of England, and so ends up a little like the mother country. But its green and pleasant land is scarred with the remnants of its gloomy penal past: the gutted gray buildings at Port Arthur, the graves on the Isle of the Dead, and all the other grisly mementos of a place once known as "Hell on Earth."

By contrast, the social history of modern Australia—and of many places like it—is summarized most tidily in the main shopping street in Adelaide, the wondrously compact little town laid out in a square by a man named Light. The thoroughfare begins life as Hindley Street, a rough-and-tumble desolation row of sailors' haunts—video arcades, take-away joints, and tawdry souvenir shops. The names say it all: the Box Adult Book Shop, Joynt Venture smoking paraphernalia, For Roses Tattoo Studio, the Sweetheart cocktail lounge, the Pop-in Coffee Lounge, and Crazy Horse Striptease Revue. Then, downtown, it turns into Rundle Mall, a gleaming, pedestrian-only monument to civic order, the sort of middling Middle Australian area you expect to find in any suburban center: Florsheim Shoes, Thomas Cook Travel, Standard Books, Woolworth's, and—on both sides of the central intersection—the Golden Arches.

Finally, on its eastern edge, Rundle Mall opens up into Rundle Street, a SoHoian anthology of today: the Appar-allel boutique, Known Space books, the Campari bistro, Al Fresco gelateria, the Australian School of Meditation, Bryan's Hairdressers, the Bangkok restaurant, Kelly's Grains and Seeds—one long neon-and-mannequin line of vintage clothes stores and veggie restaurants, culminating (as it must culminate) in the New Age Emporium. This street alone, it seems, tells the story of how the twenties became the fifties became the eighties, or how raffishness turned into Standard Shopping Center and then was reborn as Authentic Renovated and Redecorated Raffishdom.

As for the booming present tense, it is best inspected in the one area that contradicts the quiet and unpeopled air of the continent—and also, not coincidentally, the one area expressly designed for foreigners: the twenty-one-mile Floridian motel-and-minigolf seaside strip known as the Gold Coast, an hour south of Brisbane. Centered on the town of Surfers Paradise, a place as self-effacing as its name, the Coast has become a furious riot of development, disco music pulsing through its glassy new arcades, Porsches cruising along its jungle of high-rises, a seemingly unending stretch of traffic-choked boulevards littered with ice cream parlors, Spanish-style motels, and Pizza Huts. There is a wax museum here, and Kenny Koala's Dreamworld. Ripley's Believe It or Not! is scheduled to open any day. And in truth, Surfers Paradise—or should it be called Surface Paradise?—has all the wound-up frenzy of an amusement park writ huge, a neo–Atlantic City tricked up in *Miami Vice* colors and high-tech accessories. Nothing is missing here, it seems, except surfers, perhaps, and paradise.

Amidst the hustle-bustle of the Gold Coast, you can even get a glimpse into the future tense of Australia and of many other outposts of the Japanese empire. Huge toy koalas sit on sidewalks, cradling hard-sell messages in katakana script. Japanese honeymoon couples, identified by their matching outfits (or their HOMEY HONEYMOON T-shirts), crowd into pink coffee shops and "Love Buses." Neon signs flicker above prices in yen, and even male strip shows couch their ads in terms guaranteed to please wholesome visitors from Kansai—"Revealing, Naughty, but Nice." What used to be the Holiday Inn is now the All Nippon Airways Hotel, and the most famous koala sanctuary in all Australia, Lone Pine, is now owned by Kamori Kanko Ltd. Even in the distant town of Cairns, desultory koto music drifts around the malls.

In the end, though, the greatest marvels of Australia reside simply in its land—the silence and the sky. For more than a day, you can travel through the Outback, a parched white land of ghosts, of blanched trees twisted at odd angles across a plain as vast and mysterious as Africa. Nothing breaks the vacancy but a dead cow, an upturned car, a stray eagle. Everywhere there is only emptiness and flatness. And then, rising up unanswerably against a diorama-bright landscape of shocked blue and thick red, Ayers Rock, old and mute and implacable, in powerful counterpoint to the young, pretty, somewhat uninflected society all around. The sacred rock is one of those rare places with a genuine sense of mystery: it casts a larger shadow than any postcard could suggest.

Or awaken one Edenic morning in Kakadu to see the sun gilding the swampy billabong, jackaroos hovering above the water in the golden, gauzy early light. Two hours later, on the South Alligator River, listen to a guide reciting names as if riffling through the multicolored pages of some children's picture book: pelicans and egrets and snakebirds are here; pied herons, masked plovers, and migrant warders from Siberia; lotus birds are among the mango trees, and white-breasted sea eagles (with a wingspan of six feet), glossy ibises (with sickle-shaped beaks), and whistling ducks ("not capable of quacking"). There are blue-winged kookaburras in the sky, and sulphur-crested cockatoos; frill-necked lizards along the riverbank, and even lazy crocodiles sunbathing just ten feet from the boat. At dusk, the birds honk and squawk above a huge, pink-flowering lily pond, and flocks of black magpie geese and silver-winged corellas fly across the face of a huge full moon that sits in the middle of the darkening sky, catching the silver of their wings. In the daily enchantment of dusk, a visitor begins, at last, to catch the presence of an Australia within, a *terra incognita* deep inside, and a loneliness that will stay with him even when he leaves. In the twilight of Australia, the foreigner can catch an intimation of what Melville calls "the great America on the other side of the sphere," and so a sense of how everything brings him back to the natural state where he began: a lonely person in a Lonely, Lonely Place.